Excel® 2003 Just the Steps™

FOR

DUMMIES®

by Diane Koers

WILEY

Wiley Publishing, Inc.

Excel® 2003 Just the Steps™ For Dummies®

Published by
Wiley Publishing, Inc.
111 River Street
Hoboken, NJ 07030-5774
www.wiley.com

Copyright © 2006 by Wiley Publishing, Inc., Indianapolis, Indiana

Published by Wiley Publishing, Inc., Indianapolis, Indiana

Published simultaneously in Canada

For general information on our other products and services, please contact our Customer Care Department within the U.S. at 800-762-2974, outside the U.S. at 317-572-3993, or fax 317-572-4002.

For technical support, please visit www.wiley.com/techsupport.

Wiley also publishes its books in a variety of electronic formats. Some content that appears in print may not be available in electronic books.

Library of Congress Control Number: 2005938248

ISBN-13: 978-0-7645-7488-7

ISBN-10: 0-7645-7488-4

Manufactured in the United States of America

10 9 8 7 6 5 4 3

1B/SU/QT/QW/IN

WILEY

About the Author

Diane Koers owns and operates All Business Service, a software training and consulting business formed in 1988 that services the central Indiana area. Her area of expertise has long been in the word-processing, spreadsheet, and graphics area of computing as well as providing training and support for Peachtree Accounting Software. Diane's authoring experience includes over thirty books on topics such as PC Security, Microsoft Windows, Microsoft Office, Microsoft Works, WordPerfect, Paint Shop Pro, Lotus SmartSuite, Quicken, Microsoft Money, and Peachtree Accounting, many of which have been translated into other languages such as Dutch, Bulgarian, Spanish, and Greek. She has also developed and written numerous training manuals for her clients.

Diane and her husband enjoy spending their free time fishing, traveling, and playing with their four grandsons and Little Joe, their Yorkshire Terrier.

Dedication

To Daniel Scott, a very precious and long awaited addition to our family!

Author's Acknowledgments

I am deeply thankful to the many people at Wiley Publishing who worked on this book. Thank you for all the time you gave and for your assistance.

To Bob Woerner, for the opportunity to write this book and his confidence in me. A very special thank you to Pat O'Brien for his assistance (and patience) in the book development; to Rebecca Senninger for keeping me grammatically correct, and to Bill Moorehead for checking all the technical angles. And, last but certainly not least, a *big* thank you to Maridee Ennis and all those behind the scenes who helped this book become a reality. It's been an interesting experience.

Publisher's Acknowledgments

We're proud of this book; please send us your comments through our online registration form located at www.dummies.com/register/. Some of the people who helped bring this book to market include the following:

Acquisitions, Editorial, and Media Development

Project Editor: Pat O'Brien

Acquisitions Editor: Bob Woerner

Copy Editor: Rebecca Senninger

Technical Editor: Bill Moorehead

Editorial Manager: Kevin Kirschner

Media Development Manager: Laura VanWinkle

Editorial Assistant: Amanda Foxworth

Cartoons: Rich Tennant (www.the5thwave.com)

Composition Services

Project Coordinator: Maridee Ennis

Layout and Graphics: Denny Hager, Melanee Prendergast, Heather Ryan, Erin Zeltner

Proofreaders: Leeann Harney, Betty Kish

Indexer: Ty Koontz

Publishing and Editorial for Technology Dummies

Richard Swadley, Vice President and Executive Group Publisher

Andy Cummings, Vice President and Publisher

Mary Bednarek, Executive Acquisitions Director

Mary C. Corder, Editorial Director

Publishing for Consumer Dummies

Diane Graves Steele, Vice President and Publisher

Joyce Pepple, Acquisitions Director

Composition Services

Gerry Fahey, Vice President of Production Services

Debbie Stailey, Director of Composition Services

Contents at a Glance

Welcome to the world of Microsoft Excel, the most popular and powerful spreadsheet program in the world. You may ask...what is a spreadsheet program? A spreadsheet is a computer program with a huge grid designed to display data in rows and columns where you can create calculations to perform mathematical, logical, and other types of operations on the data you enter. You can sort the data, enhance it, and manipulate it a plethora of ways including creating powerful charts and graphs from it. Whether you need a list of names and addresses, or a document to calculate next year's sales revenue based on prior years' performance, Excel is the application you want to use.

About This Book

This book provides the tools you need to successfully tackle the potentially overwhelming challenge of using Microsoft Excel. Through this book you find out how to create spreadsheets; however, what you create is totally up to you. Your imagination is the only limit!

Why You Need This Book

Time is of the essence and most of us don't have the time to do a lot of reading. We just need to get a task done, effectively and efficiently. This book is full of concise, easy to understand steps designed to get you quickly up and running with Excel by taking you directly to the steps for a desired task, without all the jibber-jabber that often accompanies other books.

How This Book Is Organized

This book is divided into eighteen different chapters broken into five convenient parts:

Part 1: Putting Excel to Work

In Chapter 1, you uncover the basics of working with Excel files, such as opening, closing, and saving files, while in Chapter 2, you work with entering the

Introduction

Conventions used in this book

➡ When you have to type something, I put it in **bold** type.

➡ For menu commands, I use the ⇨ symbol to separate menu items. For example, choose File⇨Open. The ⇨ symbol is just my way of saying "Choose Open from the File menu."

 This icon points out insights or helpful suggestions related to the tasks in the step list.

different types of data into Excel worksheets, and in Chapter 3, you create various types of formulas and functions to perform worksheet calculations.

Part II: Sprucing Up Your Spreadsheet

Chapter 4 shows you how to dress up the data you enter into a worksheet, including data alignment, formatting values, changing fonts, colors, and cell borders. In Chapter 5, you also work with graphics such as arrows and clip art. Then in Chapter 6, you work with multiple worksheets, hyperlinks and worksheet protection, and passwords.

Part III: Viewing Data in Different Ways

This part shows how you modify how Excel displays certain workbook options on your screen. Chapter 7 illustrates changing the worksheet views. In Chapter 8, you sort your data making it easier to locate particular pieces of information. In Chapter 9, you create charts to display your data in a superb graphic manner and in Chapter 10 you work with the different output methods, including printing, for your worksheets.

Part IV: Analyzing Data with Excel

Use these chapters to effectively analyze all the data you input into a worksheet. In Chapters 11, 12, and 13, you work with Excel Outlines, Filters, and Pivot Tables. Chapters 14 and 15 show some of the timesaving data entry tools included with Excel.

Part V: Practical Applications for Excel

Go to these chapters to save yourself time with a commission calculation worksheet (Chapter 16), a medical expense tracking worksheet (Chapter 17), and Chapter 18 which helps you plan for your future by planning to purchase a house, pay off a credit card balance, and save for college or retirement. Chapters 19 through 21 show how you can use Excel with the other Office programs — Word, Powerpoint, and Access.

Part I
Putting Excel to Work

The 5th Wave   By Rich Tennant

Working with Excel Files

*Y*our PC probably has many different computer programs loaded on it, but you'll not likely find one that is as versatile as Microsoft Excel. Throughout the course of this book, you discover methods to use Excel as a spreadsheet of course, but also as a database, a calculator, a planner, and even a graphic illustrator. But as with most things in life, you need to figure out the basics before you can carry out the more advanced actions.

In this chapter, you

➡ Discover the fundamental measures needed when working with Excel files; basic operations to file management such as opening, closing, and saving files.

➡ Meet Clippit, the animated Office Assistant, who stands by your virtual screen waiting for a question from you. Clippit takes your question to the Excel Help system, both local and over the Internet, searching to provide the best answer to your inquiry.

➡ Customize what you see on the Excel screen, thereby making it easier and faster for you to use.

➡ Use workbook properties to better manage your files and provide a means to search for those files that sometimes mysteriously get lost in a computer hierarchy.

Get ready to. . .

Open and Close Excel

1. To open Excel, choose Start⇨All Programs⇨Microsoft
    Office⇨Microsoft Excel. The Microsoft Excel program
    begins with a new blank workbook, as shown in
    Figure 1-1, ready for you to enter data. Take note of
    the following elements on-screen:

    - **Getting Started task pane:** Appears on the right side
      on the workbook.

    - **Office Assistant:** An animated icon that can answer
      questions, offer tips, and provide help. See the "Use
      the Office Assistant" section later in this chapter.

    - **Toolbars:** A series of tools that provide fast access
      to commonly used Excel features. By default, Excel
      includes nineteen toolbars but only three display
      when you start Excel: Standard, Formatting, and
      Drawing. See "Separate the Toolbars" and "Display
      Different Toolbars" later in this chapter.

    If you have an Excel icon on your Windows desktop, double-click
    the icon for a quick way to start Excel.

2. To close the current workbook, choose File⇨Close. If any
    changes are not saved, Excel prompts you to save your
    changes. See "Save a Workbook" later in this chapter.

    Optionally, click the Close box to close the current Excel file. If no
    other workbook is open, the Excel program also closes.

3. To exit Excel, choose File⇨Exit as shown in Figure 1-2.
    The Excel file and program closes. If any changes are not
    saved, Excel prompts you to save your changes.

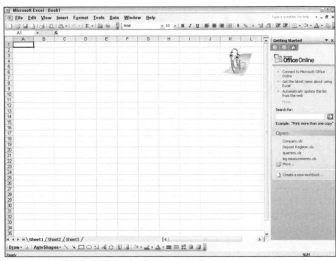

Figure 1-1: A blank Excel workbook that Excel calls Book1

Figure 1-2: Closing Excel releases the program from your computer memory

Create a New Excel File

1. Choose File➪New. The New Workbook options appear on the task pane.

   Optionally, press Ctrl+N or click the New button on the toolbar to create a new blank workbook.

2. From the task pane, click Blank Workbook. A new workbook (see Figure 1-3) appears on top of the existing workbook.

Save a Workbook

1. Choose File➪Save or click the Save button on the toolbar. The Save As dialog box appears, as shown in Figure 1-4.

   Optionally, press Ctrl+S to save the Excel file.

2. By default, Excel saves your files in the My Documents folder. If you want to save your file in a different folder, select the folder where you want to save the file from the Save In drop-down list.

3. In the File Name text box, type a descriptive name for the file.

   Filenames cannot contain an asterisk, slash, backslash, or the question mark character.

4. Click the Save button. Excel saves the workbook in the location and with the name you specified.

Figure 1-3: Excel calls each new workbook by the next increment

Figure 1-4: The Excel Save As dialog box

Open an Existing Excel File

1. With Excel already open, choose File⇨Open or click the Open button on the toolbar. The Open dialog box opens, as shown in Figure 1-5.

    Optionally, press Ctrl+O to display the Open dialog box.

    At the bottom of the File menu, Excel stores the names of the last four Excel files you opened. Click any listed filename to quickly open the selected file.

2. By default, Excel looks for your files in the My Documents folder. If your file is not in My Documents, select the appropriate folder from the Look In drop-down list.

3. Select the file you want to open.

4. Click the Open button. Excel opens the file.

Delete an Existing Excel File

1. With Excel open, choose File⇨Open or click the Open button on the toolbar. The Open dialog box displays.

2. Right-click the file you want to delete. Do not open the file.

3. Choose Delete from the shortcut menu (see Figure 1-6). A confirmation message appears.

4. Click Yes. Excel deletes the file.

5. Click the Cancel button to close the Open dialog box.

Figure 1-5: Use the Open dialog box to locate a previously saved Excel file

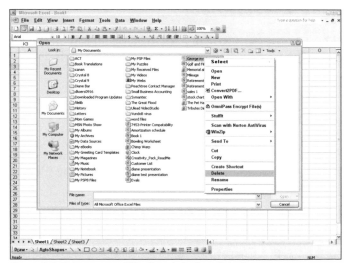

Figure 1-6: Delete unwanted files through the Open dialog box.

Use the Office Assistant

1. Click anywhere on the Office Assistant icon. The Office Assistant displays a What Would You Like to Do text box.

    Want to see your Office Assistant do tricks? Right-click the assistant and select Animate. Each different Office Assistant performs a different series of tricks.

2. Type a request in the text box, as shown in Figure 1-7. Then, press Enter.

3. The results of your request appear in a Search Results task pane on the right side of your screen (see Figure 1-8). Click any link in the Search Results task pane to discover the answer to your request.

4. Optionally, drag the Office Assistant to a different part of your screen if it's in your way. In many cases, the Office Assistant moves out of the way automatically.

    Right-click the Office Assistant and select Choose Assistant, which displays the Office Assistant dialog box. From the Gallery tab, you can select a different assistant than the default paper clip. Options include a robot, a magician, a cat, a dog, and others.

5. Click the Close box in the upper-right corner of the Search Results task pane to put it away.

6. Right-click the Office Assistant and choose Hide to temporarily hide the Office Assistant.

    To permanently hide the Office Assistant, right-click the Office Assistant, choose Options, and remove the check mark from the Use the Office Assistant option.

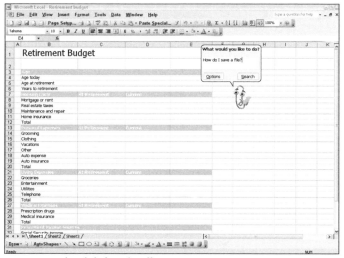

Figure 1-7: Asking help from the Office Assistant

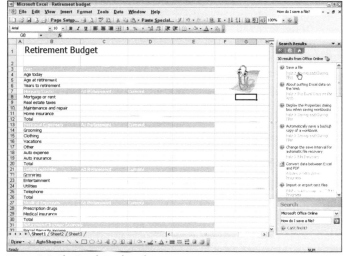

Figure 1-8: The Search Results task pane

Separate the Excel Toolbars

1. Choose View➪Toolbars➪ Customize. The Customize dialog box appears.

2. Click the Options tab (see Figure 1-9).

3. Select the Show Standard and Formatting Toolbars on Two Rows option. Excel displays the toolbars separately, which makes the most commonly used tools easily accessible.

4. Click the Close button.

 In the Customize dialog box, select the Always Show Full Menus to immediately display all the menu choices when you click a menu such as File or View. With this option unchecked, you must click the down arrow on a menu to display the remainder of the options.

Figure 1-9: Display the Standard and Formatting toolbars in their entirety

Display Different Toolbars

1. Choose View➪Toolbars. Toolbars currently displayed have a check mark next to them. (See Figure 1-10.)

2. Select a toolbar you want to display. A few of the tool-bars are

   - **Standard:** See Chapters 1, 7, 9, 10, and 12.

   - **Formatting:** See Chapters 4, 5, and 8.

   - **Drawing:** See Chapters 5 and 9

   - **Chart:** See Chapter 9

   - **Picture:** See Chapter 5

3. Repeat Steps 1 and 2 to hide a toolbar from display.

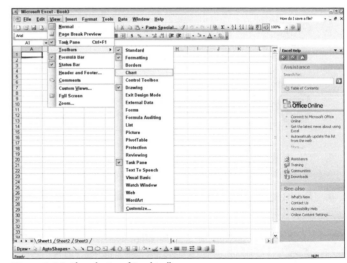

Figure 1-10: The selection of Excel toolbars

Specify Workbook Properties

1. Choose File⇨Properties. The Properties dialog box appears with several tabs:

   - **General:** Illustrates filename, location, size, and dates including the creation, modification, and last accessed date. Excel automatically updates the information on the General tab.

   - **Summary:** Includes fields for author, title, subject, and other similar information. (See Figure 1-11.)

   - **Custom:** Allows you to create custom fields that you can assign text, date, number, or even yes or no values (see Figure 1-12).

   - **Statistics:** Displays facts about the workbook usage including creation, modification and last print date, editing time, and revision numbers.

   - **Contents:** Displays a list of all worksheets included in the workbook.

    To have Excel automatically prompt you to set file properties for every workbook you create, choose Tools⇨Options and on the General tab, select the Prompt for Workbook Properties check box. When you save a workbook the first time, Excel displays the Properties dialog box.

2. Select the tab on which you want to enter information and enter any desired data.

3. Click OK.

4. Save the workbook. The workbook properties are saved with the workbook data.

Figure 1-11: Search for workbooks based on information stored in the Properties dialog box

Figure 1-12: Create your own summary fields

Search for a File by Properties

1. Choose File➪Open. The Open dialog box appears.

2. Click the Tools button and choose Search from the menu.

3. In the File Search window, click the Advanced tab.

4. Select the field you want to search from the Property drop-down list.

5. In the Value box, enter the data by which you want to search.

6. Click the Add button.

7. Select where to search from the Search In drop-down list.

8. Select the file types you want to look for from the Results Should Be drop-down list as shown in Figure 1-13.

9. Click the Go button. A list of the files matching your criteria appears at the bottom of the File Search window.

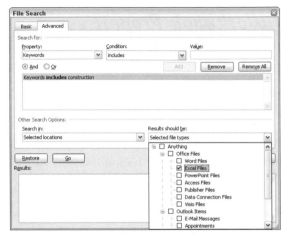

Figure 1-13: Searching for file by property values

Save or Open Files in Different Formats

1. Choose File➪Save As or File➪Open.

2. Select a location in which to save the file or the location in which your file is currently located.

3. Select the file type you want to use from the Save as Type (shown in Figure 1-14) or Files of Type drop-down list.

4. Enter a name for the file in the File Name text box or select the file you want to open.

5. Click Save or Open.

Figure 1-14: Save a workbook as a different file type

Entering Spreadsheet Data

*Y*ou can enter three primary types of data in a spreadsheet: labels, values, or formulas. Labels are traditionally descriptive pieces of information such as names, months, or other identifying statistics and usually include alphabetic characters. Values are generally raw numbers or dates and formulas are results of calculations.

The first part of this chapter shows how you can easily enter labels and values into your worksheet. But, alas, none of us are perfect and you may need to correct your mistakes. So I also show you how to delete incorrect entries, duplicate data, or move it to another area of the worksheet. You even discover an Excel feature that prevents worksheet cells from accepting the incorrect data.

Chapter 2

Get ready to. . .

Change the Active Cell

1. Open a spreadsheet in Excel. The formula bar displays the active cell location. A single worksheet has 256 columns across and 65536 rows down. Columns display the letters from A to IV and rows display numbers from 1 to 65536. A cell address is the intersection of a column and a row such as D23 or AB205.

2. Move the cursor to an adjacent cell with one of the following techniques:

   - **Down:** Press the Enter key or the down arrow key. In Figure 2-1, I've moved the cursor from E9 to E10.

   - **Up:** Press the up arrow key.

   - **Right:** Press the right arrow key

   - **Left:** Press the left arrow key.

3. To move to a cell farther away, use one of these techniques:

   - Click the mouse pointer on any cell to move the active cell location to that cell.

   - Choose Edit⇨Go To (or press F5). The Go To dialog box displays, as shown in Figure 2-2. In the Reference box, enter the cell address you want to make active, and then click OK.

   - Press Ctrl+Home. Excel jumps to cell A1.

   - Press Ctrl+End. Excel jumps to the lower-right cell of the worksheet.

   - Press Ctrl+PageDown or Ctrl+PageUp. Excel moves to the next or previous worksheet in the workbook.

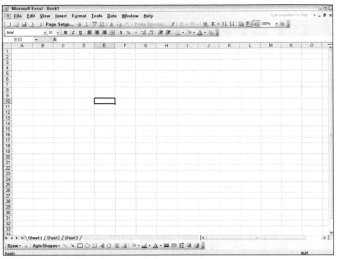

Figure 2-1: A black border surrounds the active cell

Figure 2-2: Specify a cell address in the Go To box

Enter Data

1. Type the label or value in the desired cell.

2. Press Enter. The data is entered into the current cell and Excel makes the next cell down the active cell. (See Figure 2-3.) How Excel aligns the data depends on what it is:

   - **Label:** Excel aligns the data to the left side of the cell. If the descriptive information is too wide to fit in a cell, Excel extends that data past the cell width as long as the next cell is blank. If the next cell is not blank, Excel displays only text meeting the display width. Widening the column displays additional text.

     To enter a value as a label, type an apostrophe before the value.

   - **Whole value:** Excel aligns the data to the right side of the cell.

   - **Value with a decimal:** Excel aligns the data to the right side of the cell, including the decimal point, with the exception of a trailing 0. For example, entering **246.70** displays **246.7**. The trailing zero is not lost; it simply doesn't display. (See Chapter 4 to change the display appearance, column width, and alignment of your data.)

     If a value displays as scientific notation or number signs such as in Figure 2-4, it means the value is too long to fit into the cell. You need to widen the column width.

   - **Date:** If you enter a date, such **12/3**, **Dec 3**, or **3 Dec**, Excel automatically returns 03-Dec in the cell, but the formula bar displays 12/03/2005. See Chapter 4 to change the date appearance.

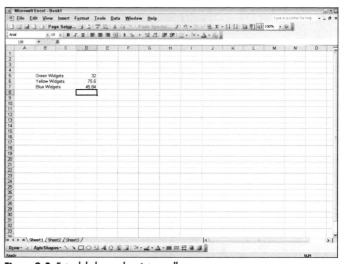

Figure 2-3: Enter labels or values into a cell

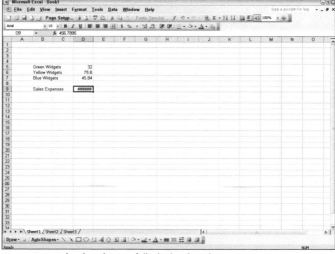

Figure 2-4: Widen the column to fully display the value

Undo Data Entry

1. Enter text into a spreadsheet.

2. To undo any actions or correct any mistakes you make when entering data, do one of the following:

   - Choose Edit⇨Undo.

   - Press Ctrl+Z.

   - Click the Undo icon on the toolbar.

3. Keep repeating your favorite undo method until you're back where you want to be.

4. To undo several steps at once, click the arrow on the Undo icon and select the step you want to undo from. (See Figure 2-5.)

 You can't undo some actions and Excel indicates this by changing the Undo command (on the Edit menu) to Can't Undo.

 To repeat the last action, choose Edit⇨Repeat, or press Ctrl+Y. You can't repeat some actions, however.

Edit or Delete Cell Data

Action	Edit
Choose Edit⇨Clear⇨Contents.	Delete the contents and retype new cell information.
Press the Delete key.	Double-click the cell contents and press the Backspace key to delete unwanted characters; then, type new characters. (See Figure 2-6.)

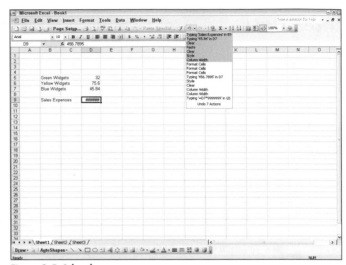

Figure 2-5: Select the steps you want to reverse

Figure 2-6: Edit cell contents without having to start over

Select Multiple Cells

What to Select	Do This
Sequential cells	Hold the Shift key and select the last cell you want to select. All cells in the selected area are highlighted, with the exception of the first cell. It looks like it's not included in the selected area, but it is. Figure 2-7 shows a sequential area selected from cell B4 to cell F15. Notice the black border surrounding the selected area.
Non-sequential cells	Hold the Ctrl key and click each additional cell you want to select. Figure 2-8 shows the nonsequential cells A4, C7, and D13 through D20 selected.
A single entire column	Click a column heading.
Multiple columns	Drag across multiple column headings.
A single entire row	Click the row number.
Multiple rows	Drag across multiple row numbers.
The entire worksheet	Click the small gray box located to the left of column A and above row 1. Optionally, you can select all cells in a worksheet by pressing Ctrl+A.

 Click any nonselected cell to clear the selection.

 Optionally, click and drag the mouse over a group of cells to select a sequential area.

 You can include entire rows and entire columns along with individual cells or groups of cells, when making nonsequential cell selections.

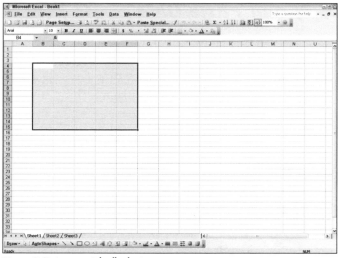

Figure 2-7: A sequential cell selection

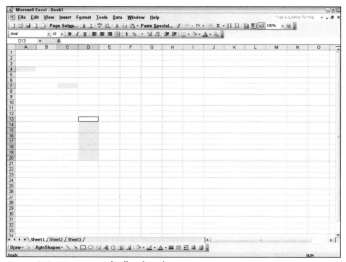

Figure 2-8: Nonsequential cells selected

Copy and Paste Data

1. Select the area of data you want to copy. The selected area is highlighted.

2. Choose Edit⇨Copy (or press Ctrl+C). The selected cells have a *marquee* (which looks like marching ants) around them (see Figure 2-9).

3. Click the cell where you want to copy the selected area.

4. Choose Edit⇨Paste (or press Ctrl+V). The selected cells are pasted into the new location.

5. Paste the cells into another location or press Escape to cancel the marquee.

 Choose Edit⇨Cut (or press Ctrl+X) and then Edit⇨Paste to move, instead of duplicate, the selected cells to a different location.

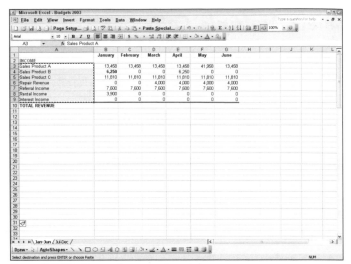

Figure 2-9: Marching ants form around a copied area

Name a Range of Cells

1. Select the cells you want to name.

2. Choose Insert⇨Name⇨Define. The Define Name dialog box shown in Figure 2-10 appears.

3. In the Names in Workbook text box, enter a name (up to 256 characters) for the range you selected. Range names are not case sensitive and must begin with a letter or the underscore character and cannot include a space or a hyphen.

4. Click the Add button and then the Close button.

 Jump quickly to a range by selecting the range name in the Go To dialog box.

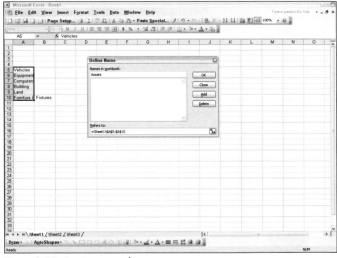

Figure 2-10: Creating a named range

Extend a Series with AutoFill

1. Type the first cell of data with data such as a day (Tuesday) or a month (August) and press Enter. AutoFill works with days of the week, months of the year, or yearly quarters such as 2nd Qtr.

2. Position the mouse pointer on the small black box at the lower-right corner of the cell. Your mouse pointer turns into a small black cross. Drag the small black box across the cells you want to fill. You can drag the cells up, down, left, or right.

3. Release the mouse. Excel fills the selected cells with a continuation of your data. Figure 2-11 shows how Excel filled in the cells with the rest of the days of the week.

 If you use AutoFill on a single value or a text word, Excel duplicates it. For example, if you use AutoFill on a cell with the word **Apple**, all filled cells contain **Apple**.

 To AutoFill a series of numbers, enter two values in two cells, such as 1 and 2. Select both cells, and then use the AutoFill box to highlight cells and Excel continues the series as 3, 4, 5, and so forth.

Locate Cells with Data Validation

1. Choose Edit⇨Go To. The Go To dialog box appears.

2. Click the Special button.

3. In the Go To Special dialog box, shown in Figure 2-12, select the Data Validation option.

4. Select All; then click OK. Excel highlights all cells that have data validation.

 To remove data validation, from the Data Validation dialog box, click the Clear All button. The following section shows how to validate data entry.

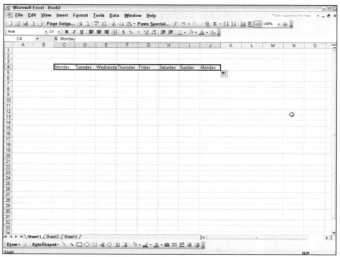

Figure 2-11: Using AutoFill for days of the week

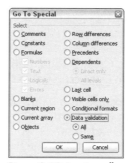

Figure 2-12: Locating cells with data validation restrictions

Validate Data Entry

1. Select the cell or cells you want Excel to validate upon data entry. Then choose Data➪Validation. The Data Validation dialog box displays.

2. From the Settings tab, choose the type of validation you want Excel to check from the Allow drop-down list:

   - **Whole Number or Decimal:** Specify the upper and lower limits of allowable data values.

   - **Lists:** Define a list, a range of cells in the existing worksheet, or a named range. (See Figure 2-13.)

   - **Dates or Times:** Specify a valid date or time ranges or limitations.

   - **Text Length:** Specify that the number of characters in the data is within the limits you want.

    When creating a list, select the In-Cell Dropdown check box if you want the choices to appear when the cell is clicked.

3. Select a criterion such as Between, Greater Than, Equal To, or Less Than or Equal To from the Data drop-down list.

4. Select other criteria such as a max and min value or specify a location for a list of data you want to allow. You can type values or refer to cell addresses. If you want to refer to a range name, precede the range name with an equal sign (=).

5. On the Error Alert tab, select an option from the Style drop-down list (see Figure 2-14) to determine whether Excel warns you about an invalid entry or stops you from entering an invalid entry.

6. Click OK.

Figure 2-13: Create a list of acceptable options or select one from the worksheet

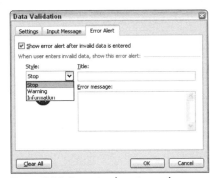

Figure 2-14: Determine the action to take upon invalid data entry

Building Formulas

*T*his chapter is all about the math. With Excel, you can create formulas to perform calculations. The calculations can be simple such as adding 2 plus 2 or they can be extremely complex such as those used to calculate depreciation. But don't despair; you don't have to do most of the work. Excel includes over 230 built-in calculations in nine different categories, which are called functions.

Functions contain arguments, which appear in parentheses following the function's name. The arguments are the details you provide to Excel indicating which numbers to calculate in the function. Some functions require several arguments to function correctly but again, don't worry; Excel contains a Function Wizard to walk you through the entire process.

The primary tasks in this chapter include

- ➡ Creating simple and complex formulas by typing them into a cell.

- ➡ Analyzing data with Excel's timesaving functions.

- ➡ Creating cell ranges separated with a colon for a sequential cell selection or by a comma to list specific cell locations.

- ➡ Evaluating formula errors and locate a cell's precedents and dependents.

Get ready to. . .

Create Simple Formulas with Operators

1. Enter values in two different cells; however, formulas do not need to reference a cell address. They can contain an actual number.

2. In the cell that you want the calculation of the two values, type an equal sign (=). All formulas begin with an equal sign.

3. Type the first cell address or type the first value you want to include in the formula. In the example in Figure 3-1, I'm adding two cell references (B5 and B6) together.

4. Using the keys on the main part of your keyboard or from the numeric keypad, type an operator. Operators include the following:

   - The plus sign (+) to add

   - The minus sign (–) to subtract

   - The asterisk (*) to multiply

   - The slash (/) to divide

5. Type the second cell address or the second value you want to include in the formula.

6. Press Enter and Excel displays the results of the calculation in the selected cell. (See Figure 3-2.)

 The formula bar at the top displays the actual formula.

 Formulas can have multiple references. For example, you could have a formula =B5+B6+B6+B8. Formulas with multiple operators are called compound formulas.

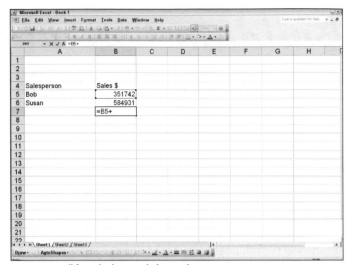

Figure 3-1: All formulas begin with the equal sign

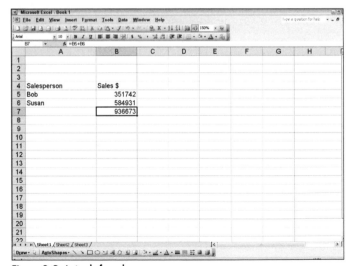

Figure 3-2: A simple formula

Create Compound Formulas

1. Type values in three or more different cells.

2. Select the cell where you want the formula.

3. Type the equal sign and then the first cell reference.

4. Type the first operator and then the second cell reference.

5. Type the second operator and then the third cell reference.

> Compound formulas are not limited to three references. They can contain many different cell references and you can use cell references multiple times in a compound formula.

6. Press Enter. Excel displays the results of the calculation in the selected cell. The actual formula appears in the formula bar as shown in Figure 3-3.

> If you were paying attention in your high school algebra class, you may remember the Rule of Priorities. In a compound formula, Excel calculates multiplication and division before it calculates addition and subtraction. This means that you must include parentheses for any portion of a formula you want calculated first. As an example, in Figure 3-4, you see where the formula $3+5*2$ gives a result of 13, but $(3+5)*2$ gives a result of 16.

> You can include range names in formulas such as =D23* CommissionRate where a specific cell was named CommissionRate. See Chapter 2 about using range names.

> Compound formulas can have multiple combinations in parentheses and can contain any combination of operators and references. A formula might read ((B5+C5)/2)*SalesTax, which would add B5 and C5, divide that result by 2 and then multiply that result times the value in the cell named SalesTax.

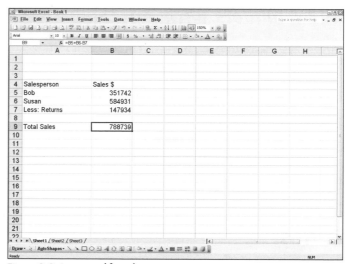

Figure 3-3: A compound formula

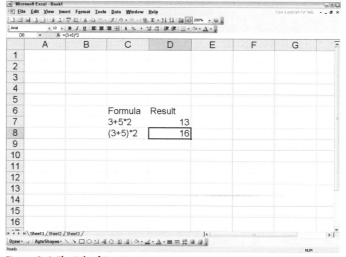

Figure 3-4: The Rule of Priorities in action

Add Numbers with AutoSum

1. Click the cell beneath a sequential list of values.

2. Click the AutoSum (Σ) button on the toolbar. Excel places a marquee (marching ants) around the cells directly above the current cell. (See Figure 3-5.)

 If the cells directly above the current cell have no values, Excel selects the cells directly to the left of the current cell. If you want to add a group of different cells, highlight the desired cells.

3. Press the Enter key to display the sum.

 The formula bar displays the actual formula that begins with the equal sign and the word SUM. The selected cells are shown in parentheses and the beginning and ending cells are separated by a colon.

Find an Average Value

1. After selecting the cell beneath a sequential list of values, click the arrow next to the AutoSum button. Besides the Sum operation, Excel displays a list of other calculation options as shown in Figure 3-6:

   - **Average:** Calculated by adding a group of numbers and then dividing by the count of those numbers.

   - **Count:** Counts the number of cells in a specified range that contains numbers.

   - **Max:** Determines the highest value in a specified range.

   - **Min:** Determines the lowest value in a specified range.

2. Choose Average and then press Enter to select the marquee. The selected cell displays the average value.

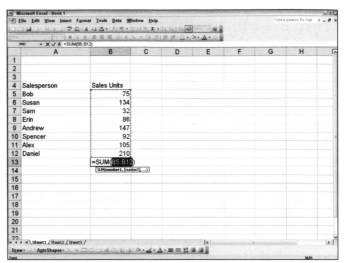

Figure 3-5: Using the AutoSum function

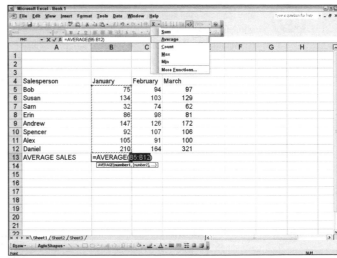

Figure 3-6: Selecting the AutoAverage function

Copy Formulas with AutoFill

1. On a cell with a formula, position the mouse on the AutoFill box in the lower-right corner. Make sure the mouse pointer turns into a black cross.

2. Drag the AutoFill box to include the cells you want to copy the formula to and then release the mouse button. (See Figure 3-7.) The AutoFill method of copying formulas is helpful if you're copying a formula to surrounding cells.

When you copy a formula, the formula actually changes because a copied formula is relative to the position of the original formula. For example, if the formula in cell D23 is B23+C23 and you copy the formula to the next cell down, to cell D24, Excel automatically changes the formula to B24+C24. If you do not want the formula to change when copied, you must make the originating formula an absolute formula (see the "Define an Absolute Formula" section coming up).

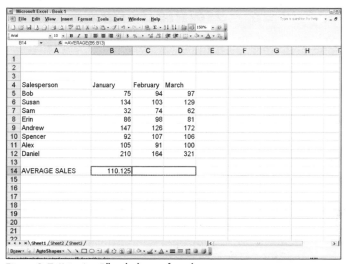

Figure 3-7: Using AutoFill to duplicate a formula

Edit a Formula

1. Double-click the cell containing the formula you want to edit (or press F2). The cell expands to show the formula instead of the result. (See Figure 3-8.)

2. Use the arrow keys to navigate to the character you want to change.

3. Delete any unwanted characters by pressing the Backspace key and type any additional characters you want to add.

Press the Delete key to delete the entire formula and start over.

4. Press the Enter key.

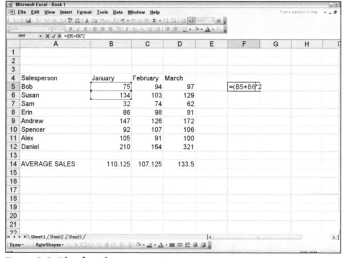

Figure 3-8: Edit a formula

Define an Absolute Formula

1. To prevent a formula from changing a cell reference as you copy it to a different location, you need to lock in an absolute cell reference by following one of these methods:

   - **Lock in a cell location:** Type a dollar sign in front of both the column reference and the row reference (for example **B2**). If the original formula in cell F5 is =E5*B2, and you copy the formula to cell F6, the copied formula would read =E6*B2 instead of =E6*B3, which is what it would read without the absolute reference. (See Figure 3-9.)

   - **Lock in a row or column location only:** Type a dollar sign in front of the column reference (**$B2**) or in front of the row reference (**B$2**).

2. Copy the formula as needed to other locations. Notice that the absolute cell reference in the original formula remains unchanged in the copied formulas.

Copy Values Using Paste Special

1. Select a cell (or group of cells) containing a formula and then choose Edit⇨Copy. A marquee appears around the selected cell.

2. Select the cell where you want the answer; then choose Edit⇨Paste Special. The Paste Special dialog box, shown in Figure 3-10, appears.

3. Select the Values option.

4. Click OK. Excel pastes the result of the formula, not the actual formula. If the original formula changes, this value doesn't change.

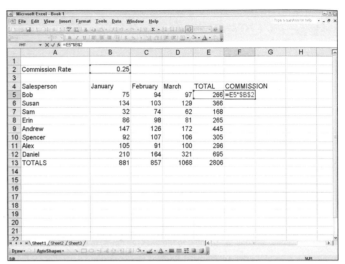

Figure 3-9: A formula containing an absolute reference

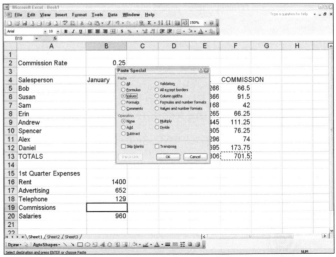

Figure 3-10: Paste only the value, not the formula with the Paste Special feature

Build a Formula with the Function Wizard

1. Select the cell where you want to enter a function; then choose Insert⇨Function. The Insert Function dialog box appears.

2. Select a function category from the Or Select a Category drop-down list. (See Figure 3-11.)

 To make the functions easier to locate, Excel separates them into categories including Financial, Date, Math & Trig, Statistical, Lookup and Ref, Database, Text, Logical, and Information. For example, the Sum function is in the Math category, while Average, Count, Max, and Min are Statistical functions. Functions that calculate a payment value are considered Financial functions.

3. Select a function name from the Select a Function list. A brief description of the function and its arguments appear under the list of function names.

4. Click OK. The Function Arguments dialog box displays. The Function Arguments dialog box you see depends on the function you select. Figure 3-12 shows the PMT function that calculates a loan payment based upon constant payments and interest.

5. Type the first argument amount or cell reference or click the cell in the worksheet. If you click the cell, Excel places a marquee around the selected cell.

6. Press Tab to move to the next argument.

7. Type or select the second argument.

8. Repeat Steps 6 and 7 for each necessary argument.

9. Click OK. Excel calculates the result based on the arguments you specified.

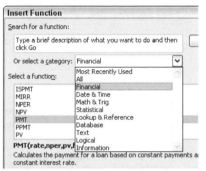

Figure 3-11: Select from over 230 built-in functions

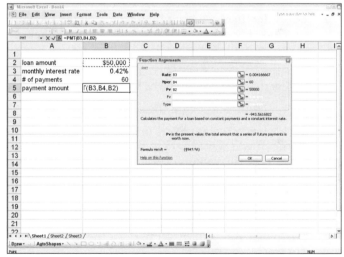

Figure 3-12: Specifying arguments for the PMT function

Generate an IF Statement Formula

1. Select a cell where you want the formula result.

2. Type the equal sign and then the word **IF**.

 You could also use the Function Wizard to help create an IF statement. Excel considers IF statements a logical function that contains three arguments. The first argument determines whether a specified condition is met. If the condition is met (or TRUE), then the function returns the value specified in the second argument; if the condition is not met (or FALSE), then it returns the values specified in the third argument.

3. Type an open parenthesis (.

4. Begin the first argument by referencing the cell you want to check. For example, if you want to check that cell B10 is greater than 100, type **B10**.

5. Type an operator such as equal to (=), greater than (>), or less than (<) and then the value you want to compare.

6. Type a comma to begin the second argument.

7. Type what you want Excel to do if the first argument is true. If you want Excel to display a value or cell value, type the value or cell reference, but if you want Excel to display text, enclose the text in quotation marks. (See Figure 3-13.)

8. Type a comma to begin the third and final argument.

9. Type what you want Excel to do if the first argument is not true.

10. Press Enter. Excel displays the results of the analysis in the selected cell. In Figure 3-14, you see the result of No in cell B8 because the payment amount was not less than the limit.

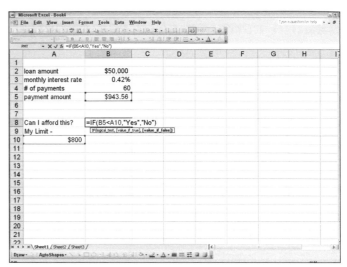

Figure 3-13: Entering IF statement arguments

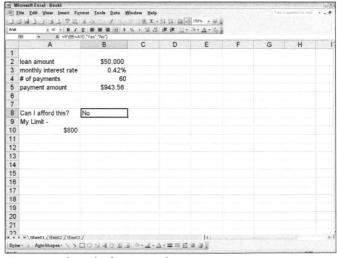

Figure 3-14: The results of a statement that was not true

Troubleshoot Formula Errors

1. Select the cell with an error message. A Smart Tag, like the one in Figure 3-15, appears.

2. Click the Smart Tag. A list of options appears. See Chapter 15 for more information on Smart Tags.

3. Depending on the error type, edit the formula as needed:

   - **DIV/0!:** Divide by zero error. This error means the formula is trying to divide by either an empty cell or one with a value of zero. Make sure all cells referenced in the division have a value other than zero in them.

   - **#VALUE!:** This error means the formula is referencing an invalid cell address. An example might be if text is in a cell and the formula is expecting a value. You may also see this error if you delete a value in a cell that was used in a formula. Locate and correct the invalid cell reference.

   - **NAME#:** This error occurs when Excel doesn't recognize text in a formula, perhaps from a misspelling of a range name. Make sure the text name actually exists and is spelled correctly. Also verify the spelling of the function name to make sure it is accurate.

   - **Circular:** This means that the formula in a cell is referring to itself. Locate the circular reference and edit the formula so it does not include itself. Figure 3-16 shows a circular reference.

 To help determine the nature of the problem or where the problem originates, click the drop-down arrow on the Smart button and click Show Calculation. Steps display the logic behind the formula.

Figure 3-15: Click the Smart Tag to display the error type

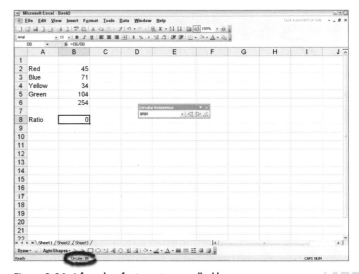

Figure 3-16: A formula referring to its own cell address

Audit Formulas

1. Choose Tools⇨Formula Auditing⇨Show Formula Auditing Toolbar. Excel displays the Formula Auditing toolbar. (See Figure 3-17.)

    Pause the mouse over each tool to see its function.

2. Select a cell.

3. To trace where formulas refer to the selected cell, click the Trace Dependents icon. Blue tracer arrows like the ones you see in Figure 3-18 appear on the screen. The arrows indicate that both cells B6 and B9 use the value in cell B2.

    Red arrows indicate cells that cause errors and a black arrow points from the selected cell to a worksheet icon if the selected cell is referenced by a cell on another worksheet or workbook.

    Dependent cells are those that contain formulas that refer to other cells. Precedent cells are those that are referred to by a formula in another cell.

4. Click the Remove Dependent Arrows icon to remove the dependent tracer arrows.

5. Select the cell that contains the formula for which you want to find precedent cells.

6. Click the Trace Precedent icon. Arrows appear indicating which cells are used in the selected formula cell.

7. Click the Remove Precedent Arrows icon to remove the precedent tracer arrows.

8. To close the Formula Auditing toolbar, choose Tools⇨ Formula Auditing⇨Show Formula Auditing Toolbar.

Figure 3-17: The Formula Auditing toolbar

Figure 3-18: Tracer arrows

Part II
Sprucing Up Your Spreadsheet

The 5th Wave   By Rich Tennant

THE TRAGEDY OF POORLY WRITTEN SLINKY DOCUMENTATION.

Formatting Cells and Data

*W*hoever said "Looks aren't everything" didn't stare at an unformatted Excel spreadsheet. Columns often aren't wide enough, fonts are too small to read, dates display in an unusual manner, and when you have columns of data stacked next to each other, sometimes the information begins to overlap.

Fortunately, Excel includes a plethora of features to make your data look more presentable and easier to read. Here are some of the Excel formatting features you'll discover in this chapter:

➡ The ability to change the font type, size and style of text, values, or dates.

➡ Change the alignment of data in a cell from the standard left aligned for text and right aligned for values or dates.

➡ Create titles using the Excel Merge and Center button.

➡ Change column width and row heights.

➡ The ability to use Excel's predefined AutoFormats.

➡ The use of styles for report consistency.

Chapter

4

Get ready to. . .

Align Data

1. Select the cells you want to align.

2. Click an alignment button on the Formatting toolbar:

   - **Left:** Lines the data along the left edge of the cell.

   - **Center:** Centers the data in the middle of the cell. If you modify the column width, the data remains centered to the new column width. Cells B4 through F4 are center aligned in Figure 4-1.

   - **Right:** Lines the data along the right edge of the cell.

 Values formatted as currency or commas can only display as right aligned.

Format Values

1. Select the cells containing values you want to format.

2. On the Formatting toolbar, click the Currency Style, Percent Style, or Comma Style button. Figure 4-2 shows values in column B, C, and D in Comma Style; column E is in Currency Style; and column F is in Percent Style.

 Cells displaying ##### indicate the cell is not wide enough to display the complete number. Widening the column displays the number.

3. To remove digits to the right of the decimal point, click the Decrease Decimal button on the Formatting toolbar. Each click removes the number to the far right of the decimal point. Click enough times and the decimal point disappears.

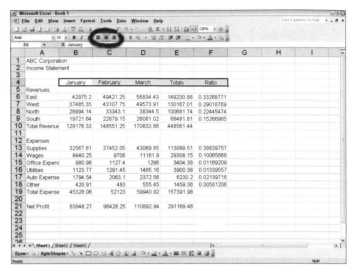

Figure 4-1: Text and values center aligned

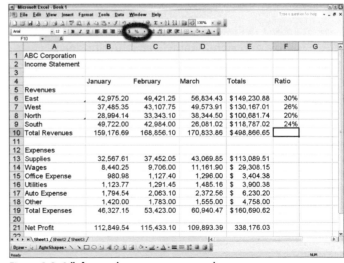

Figure 4-2: Cells formatted at currency, comma, and percentage

Indent Data in Cells

1. Select the cells you want to indent.

2. Click the Increase Indent button on the Formatting tool-bar. Notice in cells A6 through A9 and A13 through A18 of Figure 4-3 that each Increase Indent click adds a small amount of space between the cell border and the data itself. How Excel indents depends on how you format the cell:

   - **If the data is left aligned:** Excel indents to the left.

   - **If the data is right aligned:** Excel indents to the right.

   - **If the data is centered:** With the first click, Excel indents to the right, but subsequent clicks cause Excel to move the data to the left.

    Click the Decrease Indentation button to remove indentation.

Create a Title by Merging Cells

1. Select the cell containing the data you want to merge and the cells you want to include in the merge. The data cell must be in the left cell of the selection and the other cells cannot contain data as shown in Figure 4-4.

2. Click the Merge and Center button. All the selected cells merge into one larger cell and the data is centered.

    After clicking Merge and Center, you can left or right align the cell if you don't want it centered.

    Click the Merge and Center button again to unmerge the cells from each other.

Figure 4-3: Indenting helps set data apart from other cells

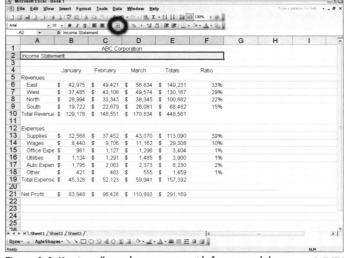

Figure 4-4: Merging cells together can create a title for your worksheet

Select Font Attributes

1. Select the cells you want to format.

2. Click the Font drop-down list. A list of available fonts appears, as shown in Figure 4-5. By default, an Excel worksheet uses an Arial 10 point font.

3. Select the font you want to use. Excel displays the selected cells in the chosen font.

4. Select the font size you want to use from the Font Size drop-down list.

5. Click any combination of the Bold, Italic, or Underline buttons on the Formatting toolbar.

 Click the Bold, Italic, or Underline button a second time to remove the attribute.

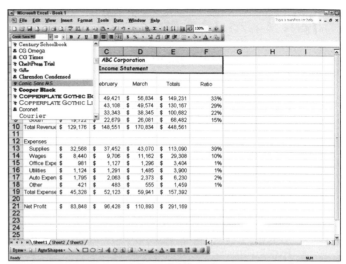

Figure 4-5: Dress up your worksheet with different fonts, sizes, and attributes

Wrap Text in a Cell

1. Select the cells you want to format.

2. Choose Format⇨Cells. The Format Cells dialog box appears.

3. Click the Alignment tab.

4. Select the Wrap Text check box from the Text Control area.

5. Click OK. In Figure 4-6, you see cells (A10 and A19) with the text wrapped.

 Selecting the Shrink to Fit option instead of the Wrap Text option allows Excel to automatically change the font size of the selected cell, which forces the data to fit in the cell's current width. Use caution with this option; the text may become unreadable.

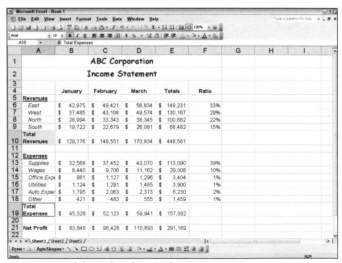

Figure 4-6: Worksheet cells with wrapped text

Rotate Text

1. Select the cells you want to format.

2. Choose Format⇨Cells to display the Format Cells dialog box.

3. On the Alignment tab, in the Orientation section, drag the small red arrow to indicate the rotation you want for your selected cells.

4. Click OK. Figure 4-7 shows cells (B4 through D4) with text rotation.

Work with Date Formats

1. Select the cells you want to format.

2. Choose Format⇨Cells to display the Format Cells dialog box.

3. Click the Number tab. As you see in Figure 4-8, you can select many different value formats.

4. Click Date.

5. Select a date format from the Type list. Notice how the sample box displays how your data will look with the selected formatting.

 If none of the date styles are what you want, you can create a custom date by clicking Custom from the Category list. Then in the Type box, type how you want the date displayed. Use **m** for month, **d** for day, and **y** for year. If you type **m**, Excel displays the month number. If you type **mm**, Excel displays the month number with a leading zero. If you type **mmm**, Excel displays the month in abbreviated form such as **Feb**. If you type **mmmm**, Excel displays the month spelled out in its entirety (**February**). Keep an eye on the Sample box to view how Excel displays the customized date formats.

6. Click OK to apply the format.

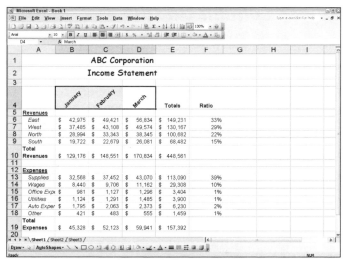

Figure 4-7: Rotating text adds a special effect to your worksheet

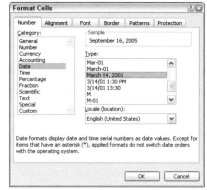

Figure 4-8: Applying date formatting

Adjust Column Width

1. Highlight the columns you want to change.

2. Choose a method to adjust column width:

   - To manually change the width of one column, position the mouse on the right boundary of the column heading until the mouse turns into a black bar with arrowheads pointing right and left. Drag the boundary bar left or right until the column is the width that you want. In Figure 4-9, I've expanded column A.

   - To set column width to a specific setting, click anywhere in the column you want to modify, and then choose Format⇨Column⇨Width. The Column Width dialog box, shown in Figure 4-10, appears. Type the exact width you want; then click OK.

    Excel displays cell width in characters and pixels instead of in inches.

   - To automatically change the width of the column so it fits the widest entry in the column, double-click the boundary on the right side of the column heading or select the columns; then choose Format⇨ Column⇨AutoFit Selection.

    The default column width is 8.43. To change the default column width on the current worksheet, choose Format⇨Column⇨Standard Width. Enter the new width; then click OK. All columns, not already manually changed, change to the standard width you specified.

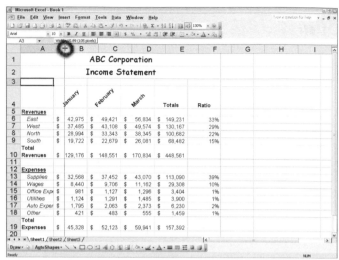

Figure 4-9: Manually changing column width

Figure 4-10: Set a specific column width

Change Row Height

1. Highlight the rows you want to change.

    Optionally, select the rows and choose Format⊏>Row⊏>AutoFit.

2. Choose a method to adjust row height:

   - To manually change the height of a single row, position the mouse on the boundary under the row heading until the mouse turns into a black bar with arrowheads pointing up and down. Drag the boundary bar until the row is the height that you want. In Figure 4-11, I expanded row 10.

      Row height is measured in points and depends on the font you are using. The default font of Arial 10 point, uses a default row height of 12.75, but Excel automatically adjusts the row height when you select a font larger than the cell height.

   - To set row height to a specific setting, click anywhere in the row you want to modify or highlight the desired rows; then choose Format⊏>Row⊏>Height. The Row Height dialog box opens, as shown in Figure 4-12. Type the exact height you want; click OK. The row changes to the height you specified.

   - To automatically change the height of the row so it fits the tallest entry in the row, double-click the boundary on the bottom of the row heading.

      The square to the left of column A and above row 1 is called the Select All square. To change the row height for all rows in the worksheet, click the Select All square and follow the steps to change all rows.

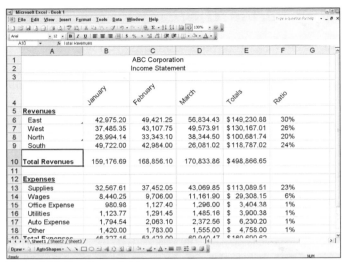

Figure 4-11: Changing row height

Figure 4-12: Enter a desired row height

Copy Formatting

1. Select a cell that has formatting you want to copy.

2. Click the Format Painter tool on the Formatting toolbar. A marquee surrounds the selected cell and the mouse pointer turns into a paintbrush (see Figure 4-13).

3. Click the cells you want to format. Excel immediately applies formats such as font, size, color, borders, and alignment.

 Double-click the Format Painter tool to lock it in so you can paint additional cells without having to reselect the tool. Click the tool again to unlock it.

 To quickly copy the width of one column to another column, select the heading of the first column, click the Format Painter tool, and then click the heading of the column that you want to apply the column width to.

Use AutoFormats

1. Select the spreadsheet data.

2. Choose Format⇨AutoFormat. The AutoFormat dialog box appears.

3. Select an AutoFormat style.

4. Click the Options button. The AutoFormat dialog box expands as shown in Figure 4-14.

5. Uncheck any AutoFormat formatting options you don't want to use.

6. Click OK. Excel applies the formatting you choose to your selected data.

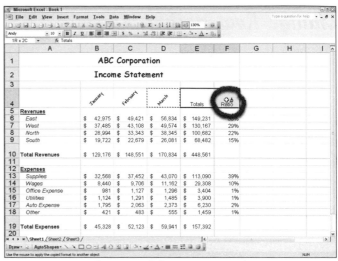

Figure 4-13: Copying formatting with the Format Painter tool

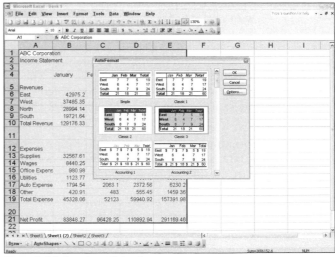

Figure 4-14: Save time with AutoFormat

Manage Formatting Styles

1. Select a cell with formatting and choose Format⇨Style. Excel displays the Style dialog box shown in Figure 4-15.

2. In the Style Name text box, type a descriptive name for the style such as **category**, **salesperson**, or **heading**.

3. Remove any check marks from the formatting categories you do not want to save with the style. You can retain any combination of formatting for a style including number style, alignment style, font style, border style, pattern style, and whether the cell is protected when the worksheet is protected.

4. Click the Add button and then click Close.

5. To apply the styles to worksheet cells, select the cells you want to have the format style.

6. Choose Format⇨Style to display the Style dialog box.

7. Select the style you want to use from the Style Name drop-down list (see Figure 4-16).

 To remove a style, select the style name and click Delete. Cells formatted with a style revert to the Normal style.

 Click the Modify button to change any of the existing format options.

8. Click OK. Excel applies the style you selected.

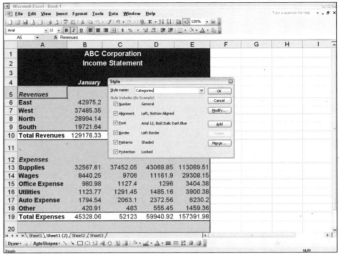

Figure 4-15: Creating a style

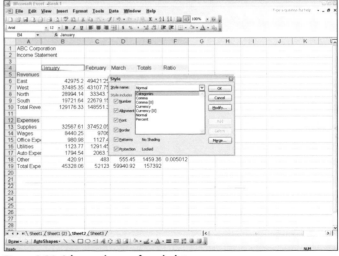

Figure 4-16: Select a style name from the list

Adding Color and Graphics

Sometimes, even after adding font and style attributes to cell data, you still need to call extra attention to specific areas. How about adding a little color to the cell data? Or instead of modifying just the data in the cell, how about making alterations such as adding a background color or a border?

And if that's still not enough, you can draw an arrow to point to a specific area. What? You can't draw a straight line? That's not a problem because with Excel, you don't have to be a gifted artist to draw. Whether you want to draw circles, squares, lines, or arrows, Excel provides tools to assist you, making the drawing process fun and easy.

In this chapter, you discover how to

➡ Add color or lines to text or cells, bringing contrast to particular portions of your worksheet.

➡ Use Excel's conditional formatting feature. With this function, you can have Excel do the legwork for you when searching for specific criteria and flag you by applying special formatting to the cells containing the criteria you're looking for.

➡ Draw arrows, shapes, and annotation boxes, all of which you can add depth to with shading and dimension.

➡ Insert clip art, which is a collection of ready-made computerized graphic illustrations, or your company logo and your viewers will sit up and take notice of your worksheet.

Get ready to. . .

Use Font Color

1. After selecting the cells you want to change the text color, choose Format⇨Cells.

2. Click the Font tab.

3. Select a color from the Color drop-down list, as shown in Figure 5-1.

4. Click OK.

 Optionally, click the Font Color icon from the Formatting toolbar (to add data color) or the Fill Color icon (to add color to the cell background).

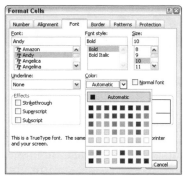

Figure 5-1: Choosing a font color

Apply Shading to Cells

1. After selecting the cells you want to add background cell color to, choose Format⇨Cells.

 Optionally, click the arrow next to the Fill Color button on the Formatting toolbar and select from a broad variety of different shading colors. Select No Fill from the options to remove any cell coloring.

2. Click the Patterns tab (see Figure 5-2), select a shading color.

 You can add a background pattern to the selected cells by selecting a fill pattern from the Pattern drop-down list. The color box under the pattern choices represent the second color used in the pattern.

3. Click OK.

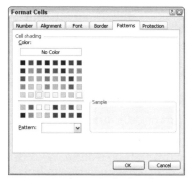

Figure 5-2: Select a color for the cell background

Place Borders Around Cells

1. After selecting the cells you want to add a border to, choose Format⇨Cells.

2. Click the Border tab. The Border tab appears (as shown in Figure 5-3).

3. Select a line style from the Style area. Choose from solid lines to dotted, dashed, or double lines. The default option is a thin solid line.

4. Select a color for the cell border from the Color drop-down list. The default color is black.

5. Select a Preset option:

   - **Outline:** Place the border around the outside of the selected cell range.

     Inside: Place the border along the inside cells of the cell range.

    You can optionally select both Outline and Inside to place a border around each individual selected cell.

6. Instead of, or in addition to the Preset options, select any of the options in the Border section to apply a border of a specific type, such as a diagonal, center, or bottom underline.

7. Click OK.

    Optionally, click the drop-down arrow next to the Border button on the Formatting toolbar. As you see in Figure 5-4, you can select from a number of predefined border styles.

    Excel also includes a Tables and Borders toolbar from which you can select border options. Choose View⇨Toolbars⇨Tables and Borders.

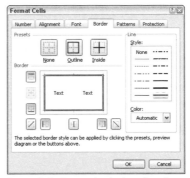

Figure 5-3: Creating border lines for cells

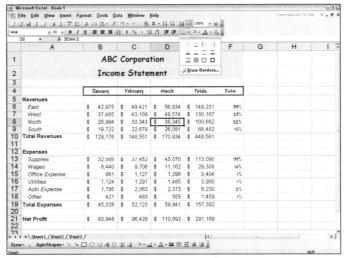

Figure 5-4: The Border button on the Formatting toolbar

Specify Conditional Formatting

1. Select the cells you want to apply conditional formatting to.

    Ideas for using conditional formatting include locating dates that meet a certain condition, such as falling on a Saturday or Sunday, specifying highest or lowest values in a range, or indicating values that fall under or over a specified amount.

2. Choose Format⇨Conditional Formatting. The Conditional Formatting dialog box, shown in Figure 5-5, appears.

3. Select the criteria you want to use from the second drop-down list in the Condition 1 area. Criteria options include Equal To, Greater Than, Less Than, and Between.

4. Enter the values you want to reference in the text box. The number of boxes depends on the condition you selected in Step 3. You can type a value here, such as 500, or you can reference a cell address, such as F13.

5. Click the Format button, which displays a modified version of the Format Cells dialog box.

6. Specify the format options you want to apply if the condition you specified is true. You can select from font styles, size, borders, patterns, or background color.

7. Click OK. A sample of your format appears in the Sample area.

8. Click OK to apply the conditional formatting or click Add to save the condition. Figure 5-6 shows formatting options applied to two cells with the specified criteria of being less than 30,000.

    To clear conditional formats as well as all other cell formats for selected cells, choose Edit⇨Clear⇨Formats.

Figure 5-5: Specifying conditions for formatting options

Figure 5-6: In this example, conditional formatting options included applying a font color change and a background color

Illustrate with Arrows

1. Click the Arrow button on the Drawing toolbar. The mouse pointer turns into a small black cross.

2. Click and drag the mouse pointer to draw an arrow, as shown in Figure 5-7.

3. Release the mouse button, and the arrow appears on the worksheet with a white circle at each end indicating the arrow is selected. (See Figure 5-8.)

    By default, Excel draws a black arrow with a thin line and small arrowhead. The arrowhead appears at the end of the drawn line.

    Click anywhere in the worksheet to deselect the arrow. Click the arrow again to reselect it.

4. Modify your arrow as needed by clicking these buttons on the Drawing toolbar:

   • **Arrow Style:** Change the arrowhead style or direction

   • **Dash Style:** Change the line style from a solid line to a dashed or dotted line

   • **Line Style:** Change the arrow thickness

   • **Line Color:** Change the arrow color

    To delete the arrow, click it and press the Delete key on the keyboard.

    See the "Manipulate Graphics" section later in this chapter to modify the arrow size, position, or direction.

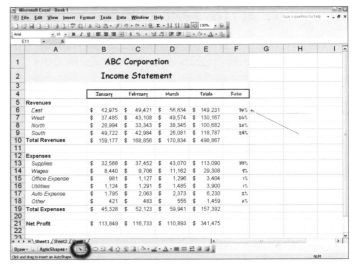

Figure 5-7: Drawing an arrow

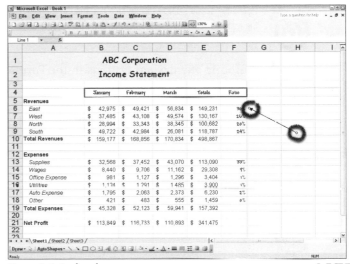

Figure 5-8: A selected arrow

Annotate with Text Boxes

1. Click the Text Box tool on the Drawing toolbar. The mouse pointer appears as an upside down cross.

2. Click and drag diagonally to draw the box the approximate size you want it. You can resize or move it later if necessary. When you release the mouse button you see a text box like the one in Figure 5-9.

3. Type the desired text.

4. Click outside of the text box to deselect it.

 Depending on the text box size and location, the text box may cover up worksheet cells. See the "Manipulate Graphics" section to see how to move it out of the way.

5. Right-click the text box and choose Format Text Box. You see the Format Text box, as shown in Figure 5-10.

 Optionally, if you want to format only a portion of the text, select the text before displaying the Format Text dialog box.

6. Select and modify any desired options in the Format Text box. Chapter 4 shows you how to use the Format Text dialog box.

 To make the text box size fit automatically around the text, select the Alignment tab in the Format Text dialog box and check the Automatic Size options.

7. Click OK.

 To delete the text box, click it and press the Delete key on the keyboard.

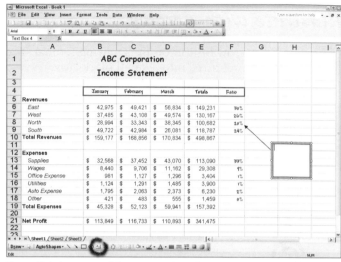

Figure 5-9: Annotate worksheet issues with text boxes

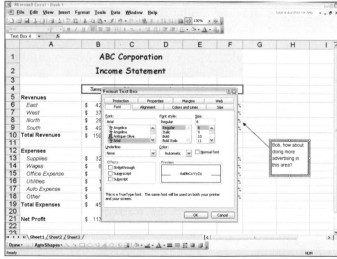

Figure 5-10: Establish options for a text box

Draw AutoShapes

1. Click the AutoShapes button on the Drawing toolbar.

2. Select an AutoShape category and then select an AutoShape (see Figure 5-11).

3. Click and drag diagonally to draw the object the size you want it; then release the mouse button.

 Select the AutoShape and begin typing to add text to the shape.

 To delete the AutoShape, click it and press the Delete key on the keyboard.

 See the "Manipulate Graphics" section later in this chapter to resize, rotate, move, or crop the AutoShape.

Shade Your Drawings

1. Select the drawn AutoShape, text box, or arrow. Click the Shadow Style button on the Drawing toolbar.

2. Select an option. As shown in Figure 5-12, the object takes on a shadowed appearance.

3. With the shadowed object selected, click the Shadow Style button again and click the Shadow Settings button. This displays the Shadow Settings toolbar.

4. From the Shadow Settings toolbar, click any button to further modify the shadowed object, such as, turn the shadow on or off; increase the shadow direction left, right, up, and down; change the shadow color.

5. Click the Close box on the Shadow Settings toolbar to put it away.

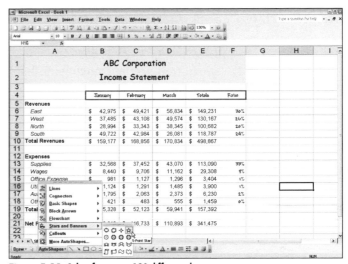

Figure 5-11: Select from over 130 different shapes

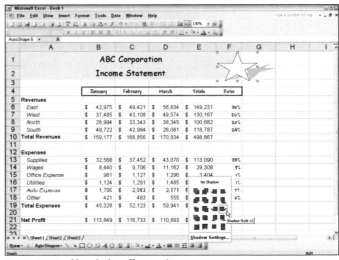

Figure 5-12: Adding shadow effects to objects

Make Objects 3-Dimensional

1. Select the drawn AutoShape or text box.

2. Click the 3-D Style button on the Drawing toolbar.

3. Select an option. The object takes on depth giving the impression of a 3-dimensional object.

4. With the object still selected, click the 3-D Style button again and click the 3-D Settings button. The 3-D Settings toolbar displays.

5. From the 3-D Settings toolbar, click any button to further modify the object (see Figure 5-13):

   - **Tilt:** Controls the object rotation up, down, left, or right

   - **Depth:** Increases or decreases the depth of the 3-D object

   - **Direction:** Changes the object perspective

   - **Lighting:** Displays the 3-D object as though a light were shining on it

   - **Surface:** Gives the object surface the appearance of solid matte to wire frame, plastic, or metal

   - **Color:** Select the object color

Insert Saved Images

1. Choose Insert⇨Picture⇨From File.

2. From the Insert Picture dialog box shown in Figure 5-14, select the picture you want to place in the worksheet.

3. Click the Insert button. Excel places the picture on the worksheet.

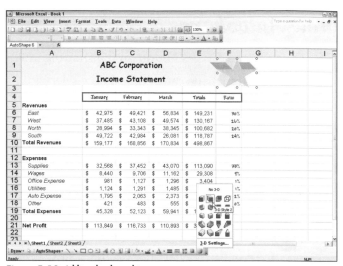

Figure 5-13: Adding depth to objects

Figure 5-14: Use this feature to insert your company logo onto a worksheet

Add Clip Art

1. Choose Insert⇨Picture⇨ClipArt. The Clip Art task pane appears on the right, as shown in Figure 5-15.

2. In the Search For box, type a brief description of the type of image you want, such as food, buildings, or people.

3. Choose where you want Excel to search for the clip art from the Search In drop-down list:

   - **My Collections:** Includes searching in your private folders such as Favorites and My Documents.

   - **Office Collections:** Includes clip art installed with the Microsoft Office application. These choices are organized by category.

   - **Web Collections:** Includes clip art from the Microsoft Office Web site.

4. Choose the type of image you want from the Results Should Be drop-down list. Excel can locate clip art, photographs, movies, or sound files.

   Click the plus sign next to any image type to further define the search options.

5. Click the Go button. Excel displays a number of images representing the art you specified, such as the images in Figure 5-16.

6. Select the desired image. Excel places the image onto your worksheet.

   See "Manipulating Graphics" later in this chapter to resize, rotate, move, or crop clip art or other images.

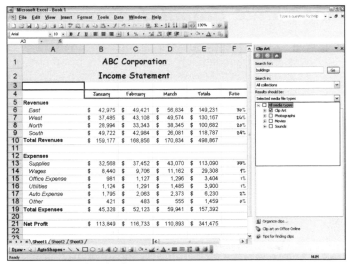

Figure 5-15: Searching for clip art

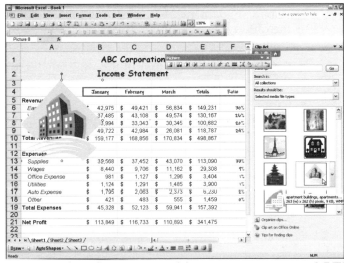

Figure 5-16: Placing clip art onto your worksheet

Manipulate Graphics

1. Select the object you want to modify. Small white circles, called *handles*, appear around the perimeter of a selected object. Arrows typically have two selection handles while other objects, including images, have eight handles. Objects other than arrows also have one small green circle called a rotation handle. Figure 5-17 shows a selected object.

2. Perform any of the following actions:

   - **Delete:** Press the Delete key on the keyboard.

   - **Move:** Position the mouse pointer over the object, but not on the handles. Click and drag the object to the desired location.

   - **Resize:** To resize an object, position the mouse pointer over one of the white selection circles and drag the circle until the object is the desired size.

   - **Rotate Shape:** Drag the green rotation handle until the object rotates to the desired angle. This does not apply to arrows.

   - **Rotate Arrow:** Drag either of the white circles in the direction you want to rotate.

   - **Crop:** From the Picture toolbar (see Figure 5-18), select the Crop tool and drag a corner, top, bottom, or side until the unwanted picture portion is removed.

    Click the Reset Picture button on the Picture toolbar to restore a picture to its original setting.

3. Click anywhere outside of the graphic to deselect it.

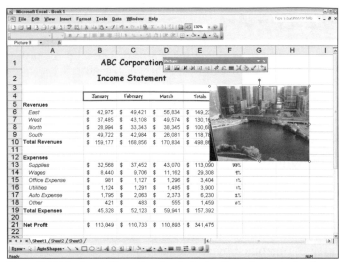

Figure 5-17: A selected object with eight selection handles and a rotation handle

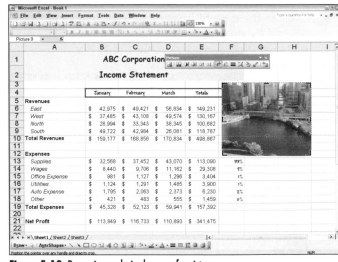

Figure 5-18: Removing undesired areas of a picture

Working with Workbooks

Allow me to begin by clearing up a couple of terms. There are *worksheets* (sometimes called *spreadsheets*), which are a single collection of cells with up to 65,536 rows down and 256 columns across. Therefore, each worksheet can contain up to 16,777,216 cells of data.

Secondly, there are *workbooks,* which are a collection of worksheets. By default, each time you create a new Excel workbook, it contains three worksheets. Each workbook however, can have up to 256 worksheets. The resulting possible number of cells in a single workbook is too huge (over 4 billion!) to even think about, but the fact remains you *could* create a single huge workbook. Realistically though, you'll probably have a number of different workbooks, each with a number of worksheets.

This chapter is primarily about working with multiple sheets. You discover how to insert, delete, move, and copy worksheets, move among the sheets, rename the tabs that reference them, and create formulas that reference other worksheets or workbooks.

It's also about protection. Throughout this chapter, you find out about security protection in the form of hiding rows, columns, single worksheets, or even entire workbooks. Discover how to lock a sheet so you or others don't accidentally overwrite critical formulas or other data. I even show you how to protect a workbook with a password so others cannot see it or modify it.

Finally, I show you how to create hyperlinks to Web sites, other cells or workbooks, or create an instant e-mail.

Get ready to. . .

Insert Additional Worksheets

1. Right-click a worksheet tab and choose Insert. The Insert dialog box appears.

 Optionally, choose Insert⇨Worksheet.

2. Click Worksheet; then click OK. Excel inserts a new worksheet. Excel names by default the first three worksheets Sheet1, Sheet2, and Sheet3, so new worksheets pick up the next number such as Sheet4. You can give your worksheet a more appropriate name. See the "Rename Worksheets" section.

3. Click a tab at the bottom of the worksheet. That worksheet becomes the current sheet (see Figure 6-1 where Sheet4 is the current worksheet).

 Optionally, press Ctrl+PageUp or Ctrl+PageDown to move between worksheets.

Delete Worksheets

1. Choose Edit⇨Delete Sheet. A warning message appears as shown in Figure 6-2.

 A worksheet with no data on it doesn't display the warning message.

2. Click the Delete button.

 You may want to save your workbook before you delete a worksheet. The Undo feature does not work with the Delete Sheet function.

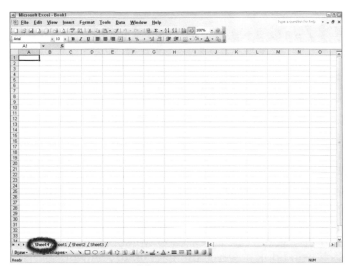

Figure 6-1: Inserting a new worksheet

Figure 6-2: Delete an unwanted worksheet

Copy Worksheets

1. Right-click the tab on the worksheet you want to duplicate. Choose Move or Copy from the menu. The Move or Copy dialog box appears.

2. Check the Create a Copy box. (See Figure 6-3.)

3. Select where, in the order of the worksheets, you want the duplicate sheet placed.

4. Click OK. Excel adds another worksheet exactly like the current one and names it with a (2) next to it.

 Select a different open workbook from the To Book drop-down list in which to place the selected worksheet.

 To quickly move sheets within the current workbook, you can drag the selected sheet tabs along the row of sheet tabs. To copy the sheets, hold Ctrl, and then drag the sheet tabs, releasing the mouse button before you release Ctrl.

Rename Worksheets

1. Click anywhere in the worksheet you want to rename.

2. Choose Format⇨Sheet⇨Rename. The worksheet tab becomes highlighted.

3. Type a unique name for the worksheet, as shown in Figure 6-4. Two worksheets in a single workbook cannot have the same name.

 Worksheet names can contain spaces and many special characters such as a dash or number sign, but they cannot contain the slash (/), backslash (\) or the asterisk (*).

4. Press Enter to accept the change.

Figure 6-3: Duplicating a worksheet

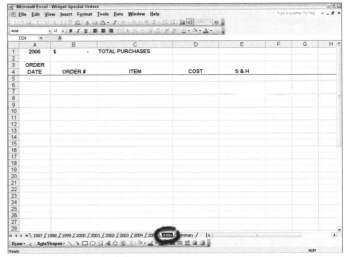

Figure 6-4: Rename a worksheet

Change Worksheet Tab Colors

1. To assist in organizing multiple worksheets, click anywhere in the worksheet you want to recolor the tab.

2. Choose Format⇨Sheet⇨Tab Color. The Format Tab Color dialog box, shown in Figure 6-5, appears.

3. Select a color.

4. Click OK.

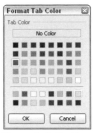

Figure 6-5: The Format Tab Color dialog box

 When a worksheet with a colored tab is the current worksheet, Excel does not display the tab color in full. It displays only a colored line under the tab name. The tab becomes full color when it is not the active worksheet.

Hide and Unhide Worksheets

1. Click anywhere in the worksheet you want to hide (hold Ctrl for multiple worksheets).

 Optionally, to hide all but one worksheet in a workbook, right-click a sheet tab and choose Select All Sheets. Then press Ctrl and click to deselect the sheet you do not want to hide. A workbook must contain at least one visible worksheet.

Figure 6-6: Select a worksheet to unhide

2. Choose Format⇨Sheet⇨Hide. Excel hides the worksheet from view. All formula references to a hidden worksheet are still valid even when a worksheet is hidden.

3. To unhide the worksheet, choose Format⇨Sheet⇨ Unhide. The Unhide dialog box, shown in Figure 6-6, appears, listing all the currently hidden worksheets in the active workbook.

4. Select the worksheet you want to unhide.

5. Click OK.

Hide Rows or Columns

1. Select the column or row headings you want to hide.

> Press Ctrl to select multiple contiguous or noncontiguous rows or columns.

2. Choose Format⇨Column⇨Hide to hide columns or Format⇨Row⇨Hide to hide rows. Notice in Figure 6-7 how column D seems to have disappeared.

> All formula references in or referring to hidden columns or rows are still valid even when hidden.

> Excel gives hidden rows a row height of 0 and hidden columns a column width of 0.

> You cannot hide selected cells. It must be an entire row or column.

Redisplay Rows or Columns

1. Select the columns before and after the hidden column, or the rows above and below the hidden row. In Figure 6-8, because column D is hidden, I selected columns C and E.

> To unhide Row 1 or Column A, choose Edit⇨Go To. In the Reference box, type A1, and then click OK. Then proceed to Step 2.

> To redisplay all hidden rows at the same time, click the small gray square above row 1 and to the left of column A, and then follow Step 2.

2. Choose Format⇨Column⇨Unhide to unhide a column or Format⇨Row⇨Unhide to redisplay hidden rows.

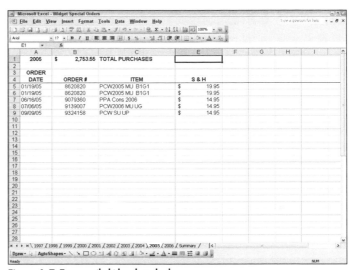

Figure 6-7: Temporarily hide selected columns or rows

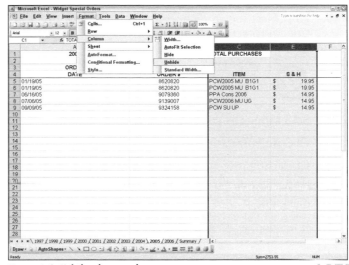

Figure 6-8: Unhide columns and rows

Unlock Cells

1. Select the cells you want to allow users to modify after you apply worksheet protection.

     When you apply worksheet protection, Excel assumes cells are locked unless you specify which cells you want unlocked. You need to unlock these cells before you apply worksheet protection.

2. Choose Format⇨Cells, which displays the Format Cells dialog box.

3. Click the Protection tab, as shown in Figure 6-9.

4. Deselect the Locked option.

5. Click OK.

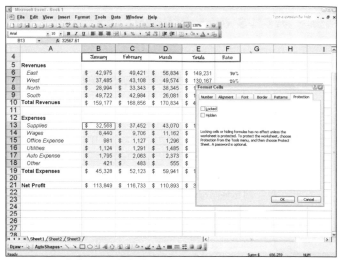

Figure 6-9: Unlocking specified cells

Relock Cells

1. Unprotect the worksheet if protected. (See the next section, "Protect Worksheets.")

     You may be prompted for a password to unprotect the worksheet.

2. Select the cells you want to relock.

3. Choose Format⇨Cells.

4. Click the Protection tab and select the Locked option (see Figure 6-10).

5. Click OK.

6. If needed, apply worksheet protection again.

Figure 6-10: Relocking cells to prevent unwanted changes

Protect Worksheets

1. Click anywhere on the sheet you want to protect. Choose Tools⇨Protection⇨Protect Sheet. The Protect Sheet dialog box appears, as shown in Figure 6-11.

    A good reason to protect a worksheet is to protect formulas from accidental changes.

2. Verify the Protect Worksheet and Contents of Locked Cells box is checked.

3. Optionally, type a password to allow a user to unprotect the worksheet in the Password to Unprotect Sheet box.

    Passwords are case sensitive.

4. From the Allow All Users of the Worksheet To box, select any options a user is allowed to change without unprotecting the worksheet.

    Deselecting the Select Locked Cells option doesn't allow an unauthorized user to even click a locked cell.

5. Click OK.

6. If you generated a password, a Confirm Password dialog box appears. Retype the password and then click OK again.

7. Try to change a locked cell in a protected worksheet. Excel displays the error message in Figure 6-12.

8. To unprotect the worksheet, choose Tools⇨Protection⇨ Unprotect Sheet. Excel prompts you to enter the password if you originally supplied one.

Figure 6-11: Protect a single worksheet

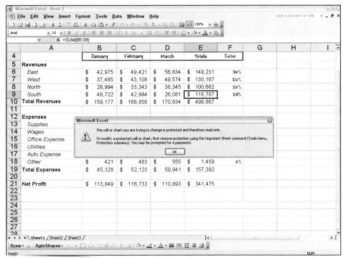

Figure 6-12: You're prevented from making changes

Create File Passwords

1. Choose File➪Save As. The Save As dialog box appears.

2. Click the Tools button and then select General Options. The Save Options dialog box appears (see Figure 6-13).

3. Type a password in the Password to Open text box if you want users to enter a password before they can even open and view the workbook.

4. Type a password in the Password to Modify text box if you want users to enter a password before they can modify the workbook. Users must have the workbook open before they're prompted for the password to modify.

5. Click OK.

6. Retype the password to open; then click OK.

7. Retype the password to modify; then click OK.

8. Click the Save button.

Click the Yes button if you're prompted to overwrite the file.

9. Open the password-protected file and the Password dialog box opens, as shown in Figure 6-14.

10. Type the password and click OK. If you opted for a password to modify, Excel prompts you for the modify password.

11. Type the modify password and click OK. The protected file opens.

To remove passwords, repeat Steps 1 through 5, but make the password boxes blank.

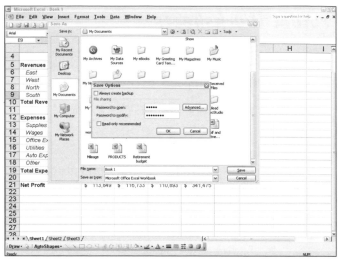

Figure 6-13: Protecting a workbook from unwanted viewing

Figure 6-14: Enter the password

Generate a Reference to Another Worksheet

1. Click the cell in which you want to create a reference.

2. To display a value located in a cell on a different worksheet, but in the same workbook, type the equal sign (=).

3. Click the worksheet tab containing the cell you want to reference and then click the actual cell you want to reference.

4. Press the Enter key. In the current cell, Excel displays the equal sign, the worksheet name, an exclamation point, and the cell reference. (See Figure 6-15.)

To display a value located in another cell on the same worksheet, type the equal sign and then the cell address; for example: **=B45**. If the value in B45 changes, the cell with the reference to B45 changes also.

Insert Cell Ref.

Include a Reference in a Formula

1. To include in a formula a cell located on a different worksheet but in the same workbook, begin the formula.

2. Click the worksheet containing the cell where you want to position the distant cell reference; then click the actual cell.

3. Finish the remainder of the formula. Figure 6-16 illustrates an example of a formula using a reference to a different worksheet.

Formulas referencing other worksheets or other workbooks can also be compound formulas or used in a function.

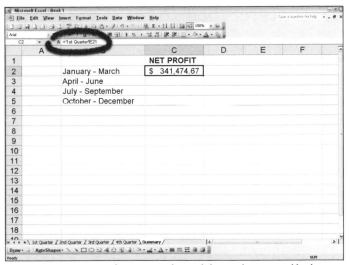

Figure 6-15: Creating a reference to another worksheet in the same workbook

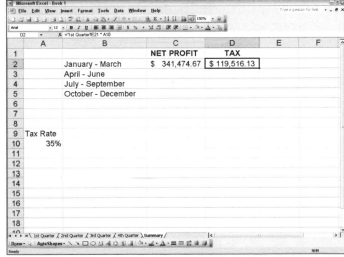

Figure 6-16: Including a reference in a formula

Cross-Reference Other Workbooks

1. Open the workbook to which you want to refer (for example, Workbook2).

2. Click the desired cell in the workbook you want to create a reference (for example, Workbook1).

3. In Workbook1, begin the formula or reference with an equal sign (=).

4. If using a function or formula, enter any portion that you want to precede the cross reference.

5. Click the cell that you want to reference from Workbook2.

6. Finish any remainder to the formula or press the Enter key. Excel displays the following: the equal sign, an apostrophe, the Workbook2 filename in brackets, the worksheet name, a closing apostrophe, an exclamation point, and the cell reference. For example, [Sales.xls]January'!E10 refers to the value in cell E10 of the sheet January in the Excel file named Sales. See Figure 6-17 for an example of a cross reference.

 Excel uses absolute references (with dollar signs) when referring to other workbooks.

7. Open the workbook that contains the cross-reference. Excel display the dialog box shown in Figure 6-18, prompting you to update the cross-referenced cell.

8. Click Update if you want Excel to check the originating workbook for changes to the referenced cell, or click the Don't Update button to leave the cell reference with the last saved contents.

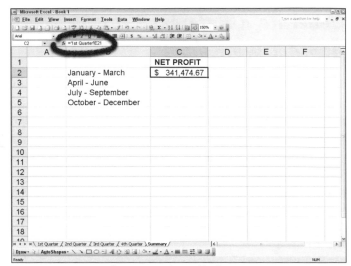

Figure 6-17: Create a reference to another workbook

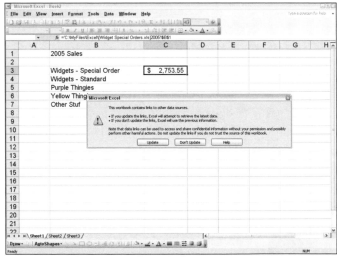

Figure 6-18: Updating a cross-referenced cell

Insert a Hyperlink

1. Select a cell or graphic object; then choose Insert⇨ Hyperlink. The Insert Hyperlink dialog box, shown in Figure 6-19, appears.

2. Select an option depending on what you want to link to:

   - **Another file:** Locate and select the filename. When the user clicks the link, the referenced file opens.

   - **A Web site:** Enter the Web address in the Address text box. When the user clicks the link, the browser opens to the referenced Web page.

   - **A different cell in the current workbook:** Click the Place in This Document button, and then specify which worksheet and cell location you want to reference. When users click this link, they're redirected to the specified cell address.

   - **An e-mail:** Click the E-mail Address button, and then enter the recipient's e-mail address and a subject. When the user clicks the link, the user's e-mail program starts (see Figure 6-20).

3. Click OK.

 To remove a hyperlink, right-click the link and choose Remove Hyperlink. The text that was entered for the hyperlink remains in the cell.

 Another method to add a hyperlink is with the Excel Hyperlink function. In the cell where you want the link, type **=HYPERLINK ("FullPathName","TextToDisplay")**. For example, if you type in cell B3 **=HYPERLINK("C:\practice.xls","Click here to open the practice file")**, cell B3 displays `Click here to open the practice file`, and when you click the link, it opens a worksheet named `PRACTICE.XLS`. Be sure to include the quotation marks.

Figure 6-19: Creating a hyperlink

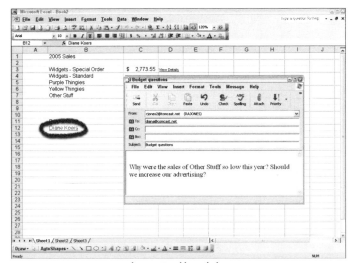

Figure 6-20: Create an e-mail via an Excel hyperlink

Part III
Viewing Data in Different Ways

Changing Worksheet Views

Someone once wrote about the importance of seeing and being seen. While I'm sure that quote referred to people, it also can apply to your Excel worksheets. You need to see them in many different contexts. That's what this chapter is about — seeing your workbook from different perspectives:

➡ Viewing alternatives such as zooming in or out, or seeing the worksheet without toolbars and other screen elements.

➡ Splitting your screen to see multiple sections of a worksheet at the same time or viewing multiple worksheets together.

➡ Freezing portions of a worksheet so you can see category or row headings.

➡ Adding non-printing comments, which are similar to sticky notes for individual cells.

➡ Quickly and temporarily hiding open workbooks — perhaps to protect them from prying eyes.

➡ Creating templates that can bring consistency, such as the company standards or personal preferences, to your workbooks.

➡ Options that change the way you view the Excel workbook. For example, see the actual formulas instead of viewing only the formula results.

Go ahead, take a look!

Get ready to. . .

Zoom In or Out

1. Choose View➪Zoom. The Zoom dialog box appears, shown in Figure 7-1.

    Optionally, click the Zoom drop-down list on the Standard toolbar.

2. Select a magnification percentage. A higher zoom setting makes the text appear larger so you see less on-screen; a lower zoom setting shows more on-screen, but the data appears smaller. Zooming does not affect the printed data size.

    You can select the Custom option and enter your own magnification percentage. Zoom values are from 10 to 400.

3. Click OK.

Split the Excel Screen

1. Click anywhere in a row and column where you want to split your screen.

2. Choose Window➪Split. Excel splits the window horizontally into two or four panes each separated from other panes, by bars. Each pane has its own set of scroll bars (see Figure 7-2).

3. Drag the horizontal split bar up or down or the vertical split bar left or right to resize the window sections.

    Choose Window➪Unsplit to remove the split or double-click any part of the bars that divide the panes.

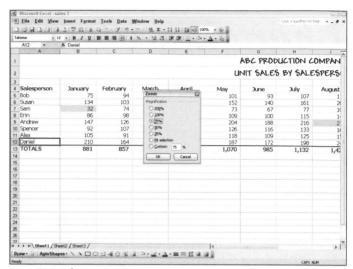

Figure 7-1: Select a zoom percentage

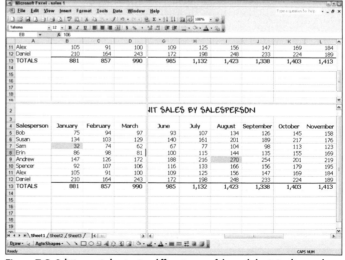

Figure 7-2: Splitting a window to view different areas of the worksheet simultaneously

Freeze Worksheet Titles

1. Choose what you want to freeze:

    - **Columns:** Select the column to the right of the columns you want to freeze. For example, click cell B1 to freeze only column A.

    - **Rows:** Select the row below the rows you want to freeze. For example, click cell A4 to freeze rows 1, 2, and 3.

    - **Columns and rows:** Click the cell below the rows and to the right of the columns you want to freeze. For example, click cell B5 to freeze both column A and rows 1 through 4 (as shown in Figure 7-3).

2. Choose Window➪Freeze Panes. A thin black line appears to separate the sections. As you see in Figure 7-4, as you scroll down and to the left, rows 1, 2, 3, and 4 and column A remain visible even though you see rows 7 through 27 in the bottom section and columns H through P on the right.

     Normally, when you press the Home key, Excel takes you to cell A1. However, when Freeze Panes is active, pressing the Home key takes you to the cell just below and to the left of the column headings.

3. Choose Window➪Unfreeze panes to remove the freeze from row and column headings.

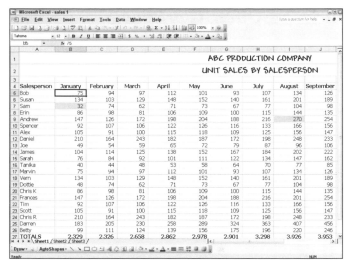

Figure 7-3: Cells above and left of the current cell will be frozen

Figure 7-4: Keep titles visible by freezing the panes

Hide an Open Workbook

1. From an open workbook, choose Window⇨Hide. The open workbook hides from view. The Excel program remains open as you see in Figure 7-5, but the workbook itself doesn't display.

     You can't find the hidden workbook name on the Window menu.

2. Choose Window⇨Unhide. The Unhide dialog box appears, displaying a list of hidden open workbooks.

3. Select the workbook you want to unhide and click OK. The workbook redisplays.Ω

Arrange Windows

1. Open two or more workbooks. Choose Window⇨ Arrange. The Arrange Windows dialog box, shown in Figure 7-6, appears.

2. Make a selection:

    - **Tiled:** The open workbooks don't overlap.

    - **Horizontal:** The open workbooks are stacked on top of each other.

    - **Vertical:** Lays the open workbooks side by side.

    - **Cascade:** Arranges the windows to overlap each other, keeping the title bar visible.

3. Click OK.

     Maximize the workbook to return it back to a larger size.

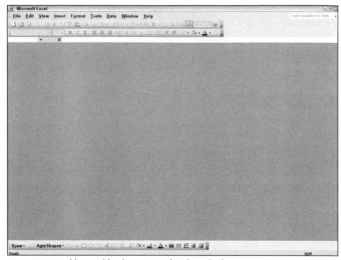

Figure 7-5: Hidden workbooks are open but don't display

Figure 7-6: Arranging to see multiple worksheets

Compare Spreadsheets

1. Open two workbooks.

2. Choose Window⇨Compare Side by Side with *other file-name*. The two workbooks are split horizontally on the screen and a Compare Side by Side toolbar appears, as shown in Figure 7-7.

3. Click the Synchronous Scrolling button to scroll the two windows simultaneously. Click the button again to scroll them independently.

4. Click the Reset Window Position button if you want to reset the workbook windows to the positions they were in when you first started comparing workbooks.

5. Click the Close Side by Side button to return the windows to normal size.

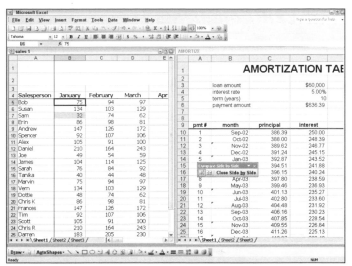

Figure 7-7: Comparing data between two different workbooks

View Excel in Full Screen View

1. Choose View⇨Full Screen. Figure 7-8 shows a worksheet in full view. Notice the title bar and toolbars are hidden. Besides the worksheet itself, only the row and column headings, the menu bar, and the Full Screen toolbar remain.

     If you want to see a particular toolbar while in Full Screen view, choose View⇨Toolbars and select the toolbar you want to use.

2. Click the Close Full Screen button to return to Normal view.

     If you closed the Full Screen toolbar, restore the screen to normal by choosing View⇨Full Screen.

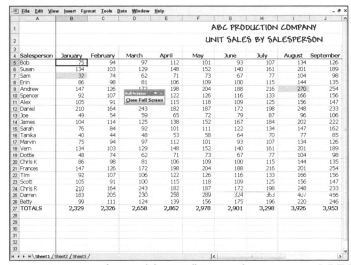

Figure 7-8: See more of your worksheet in Full Screen mode

Add Cell Comments

1. Select the cell you want to add a comment to. Choose
    Insert⇨Comment. A small red arrow appears in the
    upper-right corner of the cell with a yellow note.

2. Enter your comment text in the comment box. Format
    the text by choosing Format⇨Comment.

3. Click the mouse anywhere outside of the comment box.

4. Pause the mouse over the red triangle to read the com-
    ment. Figure 7-9 shows a comment.

 When printing the worksheet, comments do not print.

Work with Cell Comments

1. Right-click a cell with a comment. A shortcut menu
    appears.

2. Select an option from the menu (see Figure 7-10):

    *   **Show/Hide Comments:** Keep the comment visible
        on-screen.

     Optionally, choose View⇨Comments to keep comments visible
    on-screen.

    *   **Delete Comment:** Get rid of the comment.

    *   **Edit Comment:** Make any typing or formatting
        changes to the comment.

     Optionally, control how Excel manages comments by choosing
    Tools⇨Options and making a selection in the Comments section of
    the View tab.

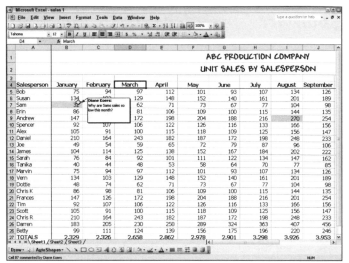

Figure 7-9: View cell comments

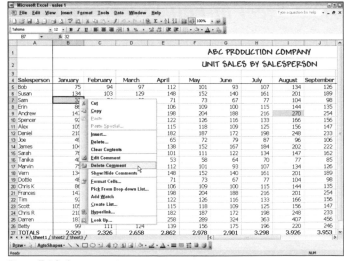

Figure 7-10: Comment options

Save as a Template

1. Create an Excel workbook. Templates can store cell, worksheet and page formats, print settings, styles, the number and type of sheets in a workbook, protected and hidden areas of the workbook, page headers, row and column labels, data, graphics, formulas, charts, data validation settings, custom toolbars, macros, hyperlinks, and workbook calculation and window view options.

2. Choose File➪Save As. The Save As dialog box appears.

3. Type a name for the template in the File Name text box.

4. Choose Template from the Save As Type drop-down list. Excel automatically saves the template in the default template location (see Figure 7-11).

5. Click the Save button.

6. Close the workbook.

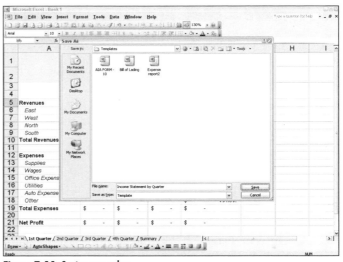

Figure 7-11: Saving a template

Open a Template

1. Choose File➪New. The New Workbook task pane opens.

 Clicking the New button on the Standard toolbar automatically creates a new blank worksheet, not from a specially saved template.

2. Click On My Computer. The Templates dialog box, shown in Figure 7-12, opens.

 Click Templates on Office Online in the New Workbook task pane to view a great collection of mostly free templates.

3. Select the template you want to use.

4. Click OK.

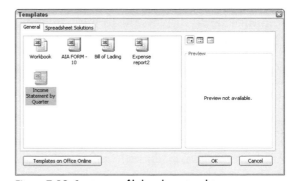

Figure 7-12: Create a new file based on a template

Customize Excel Viewing Options

1. Choose Tools⇨Options. The Options dialog box appears.

2. Click the View tab (see Figure 7-13) and then select any desired options:

   - **Show:** Select the items you see on the screen such as the formula bar or status bar. If you remove the check mark from the Startup Task Pane, Excel only displays the task pane if you select an option that requires it — such as when inserting clip art.

   - **Comments:** Determine how you want to see cell comments (see the "Work with Cell Comments" section, earlier in this chapter).

   - **Objects:** Establish whether or not to display objects such as arrows, clip art, or text boxes, or to show only a placeholder for them.

   - **Window Options:** Select the Formulas option to turn on formulas; Excel displays the formula in a cell, not the result (see Figure 7-14). This is extremely helpful when troubleshooting formula problems. Additionally, select the Zero Values option to leave the cell blank or with a dash if the cell value is zero.

Control the gridline display in the Window Options category.

Click the General tab and choose R1C1 reference style if you want Excel to display the columns in numbers instead of alphabetic characters.

3. Click OK.

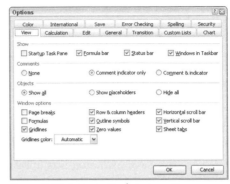

Figure 7-13: Customize Excel viewing options

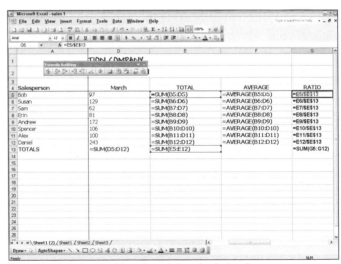

Figure 7-14: Analyze Excel formulas with formulas displayed

Sorting Data

Sometimes worksheets become quite large, which makes it time-consuming and difficult to locate particular pieces of information. If your data is in an array, you may find the data easier to view if it is sorted in a particular manner.

Perhaps you have multiple worksheets and you want to locate every occurrence of a specific value. Or, maybe you're just a neat freak and want everything to be in a particular order. Excel contains features to help keep your worksheets in an easy-to-manage sequence.

Here's what you can expect in this chapter:

- ➡ Sort your data in ascending or descending order using either the toolbar or the Excel Sort dialog box.

- ➡ Perform a secondary sort if the primary sort has multiple matches.

- ➡ Sort data containing days of the week or month names.

- ➡ Create a customized list of frequently used names or terms.

- ➡ Locate cells containing data you specify, whether the data is part of a formula or a resulting cell value.

- ➡ Quickly replace data containing certain information with another specified set of data.

- ➡ Locate all cells with a particular style of formatting and easily replace them with a different format.

Chapter

8

Get ready to. . .

Use the Toolbar to Sort

1. Create a list in contiguous order with headings specifying the contents of each column. Figure 8-1 illustrates an ideal data array.

2. Click any cell containing data in the column by which you want to sort.

     If the data is in a connected list, you do not have to select it first. If the data is not in an adjoining list, you must first select the entire list. If unselected data is in columns next to the selected data, Excel may prompt you for more information.

3. Click the Sort Ascending button. Excel sorts the entire list in ascending order. Text is sorted A–Z; numbers are sorted 1–10; and dates are sorted earliest to last.

     Excel sorts in the following pattern: numbers, spaces, special characters (which are ! " # $ % & ( ) * , . / : ; ? @ [\ ] ^ _ ` { | } ~ + < = >) and finally, alphabetic letters.

4. Click the Sort Descending button. Excel sorts the entire list by descending order, as shown in Figure 8-2. Text is sorted Z–A; numbers are sorted 10–1; and dates are sorted last to earliest.

     If you do not see two sorting buttons (Ascending and Descending), choose View➪Toolbars➪Customize and select the Show Standard and Formatting Toolbars on Two Rows option. Click the Close button and you can see both the Ascending and Descending Sort buttons.

     If Excel incorrectly sorts a cell that contains a value, make sure the cell is formatted as a number and not as text.

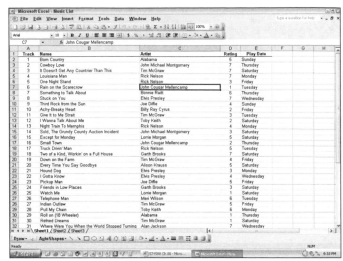

Figure 8-1: Data for sorting

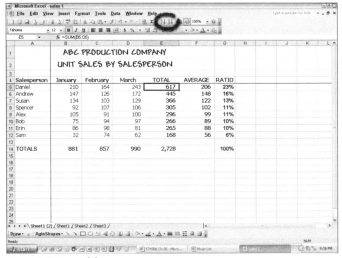

Figure 8-2: A sorted data array

Work with the Sort Command

1. Select or click in the list of data you want to sort. Select only a single column of data if you want to sort that column independently of the rest of the data.

2. Choose Data⇨Sort. The Sort dialog box opens (see Figure 8-3).

3. If your data includes column headings, select the Header Row option in the My Data Range Has section. If it doesn't include column headings, select the No Header Row option. Excel does not include header rows in the sort process.

4. From the Sort By drop-down list, select the column by which you want to sort (see Figure 8-4).

     If you do not have header rows, Excel displays Column A, Column B, and so forth.

5. Select whether you want to sort the data in ascending or descending order.

     Click the Options button if you want to make the sorting case sensitive (noncapitalized words before capitals). This option is not available in PivotTable reports (see Chapter 13).

6. Click OK. Excel sorts data in the following order: numbers, special characters, and finally alphabetic characters. Blanks are always placed last.

     When sorting an outline, Excel sorts only the highest-level groups. This keeps the detail rows or columns together, even if hidden. (See Chapter 11.)

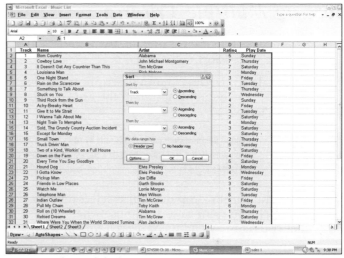

Figure 8-3: The Sort dialog box

Figure 8-4: Select the sort column

Sort by Multiple Criteria

1. Select or click in the list of data you want to sort. Choose Data⇨Sort.

2. If your data includes column description headings, select the Header Row option in the My Data Range Has section.

 Although the most common sort is to sort by rows, you can also sort by columns. In the Sort dialog box, click the Options button, choose Sort Left to Right in the Orientation section, and then click OK.

3. From the Sort By drop-down list, select the first column by which you want to sort. Choose whether to sort the first criteria in ascending or descending order.

 Excel sorts dates formatted with slashes such as 11/22/68 as numeric data. Dates with the day or month spelled out must be sorted differently. See the later section, "Sort by Day, Month, or Custom List."

4. Click the Then By down arrow and select the column you want to sort by if two or more items are identical in the first Sort By option. See Figure 8-5.

5. Choose whether to sort the second criteria in ascending or descending order.

6. (Optional) Repeat Steps 4 and 5 for a third criterion.

7. Click OK. Excel performs the sort process. Figure 8-6 illustrates data rows sorted first by Artist, and then by Song Title.

 During an Excel sort, apostrophes (') and hyphens (-) are ignored, unless two text strings are the same except for a hyphen. In that situation, the text with the hyphen is sorted as the latter.

Figure 8-5: Select a second sort criteria

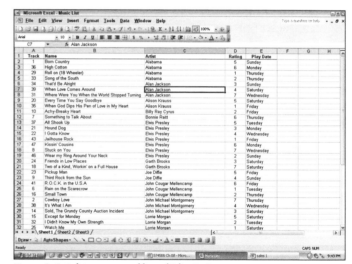

Figure 8-6: A data array sorted by multiple criteria

Create a Customized List

1. Choose Tools⇨Options. The Options dialog box appears.

2. Click the Custom Lists tab. Excel provides two ways to create a custom list:

    A custom list can contain text or text mixed with numbers. Use custom lists to speed up data entry for commonly used terms such as salespeople, regions, or products.

   - To create a list from items you already have entered into the worksheet, click the worksheet icon next to the Import button. The Options dialog box collapses. Highlight the worksheet cells containing your list; then press Enter. The Options dialog box reappears. Click the Import button. The data you selected appears in both the List Entries box and the Custom Lists box (see Figure 8-7).

   - To type your own list, without entering it into the worksheet first, select New List from the Custom Lists section. Type your list in the List Entries text box (see Figure 8-8) separating each list item with a comma, and then click the Add button.

3. Click OK.

    You can now use the AutoFill feature with the custom list by typing one list entry and using AutoFill to enter the other list entries. See Chapter 2.

    To edit a custom list, choose Tools⇨Options. From the Custom Lists tab, select the list that you want to edit. Make any desired changes in the List Entries box, and then click Add. To delete a customized list, select the list and click Delete. You cannot edit or delete the Excel provided fill series such as months and days.

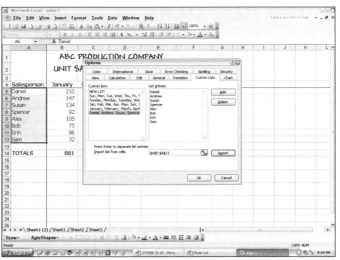

Figure 8-7: Create your own custom lists from data in your worksheet

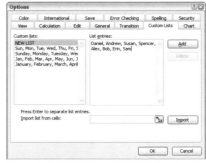

Figure 8-8: Manually create a customized list

Sort by Day, Month, or Custom List

1. Select or click in the list of data you want to sort. Choose Data⇨Sort. The Sort dialog box appears.

    Excel sorts numbers first, and then text. If your data includes values designated as text, Excel prompts you before the Sort dialog box appears how you want these cells handled. You can choose to keep the numbers as text values, or sort them as numbers. If you sort them as numbers, both numbers stored as text and actual numbers are sorted together.

2. If your data includes column description headings, click the Header Row option in the My Data Range Has section.

3. Specify the order in which you want the data sorted and whether to sort in ascending or descending order (see Figure 8-9).

    If you're sorting on days of the week or months of the year, the data must be spelled out completely (for example, September or Tuesday), or abbreviated to the first three characters only (for example, Sep or Tue).

    By default, Excel sorts days and months alphabetically instead of by date. To sort days or months by date, or to sort a custom list, the day, month, or list column must be the first sort criteria.

4. Click the Options button. The Sort Options dialog box opens.

    Unless you specify otherwise, Excel sorts customized lists alphabetically instead of list order.

5. Select a sort order from the available list. (See Figure 8-10.)

6. Click OK twice to perform the sort.

Figure 8-9: To sort days or months click the Options button

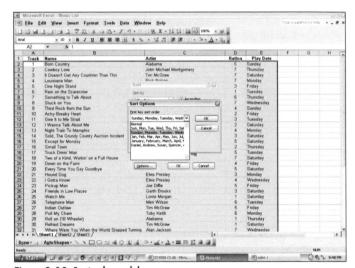

Figure 8-10: Sorting by weekday

Search for Data

1. Choose Edit➪Find (or press Ctrl+F). The Find and Replace dialog box, shown in Figure 8-11, appears.

2. In the Find What box, enter the value or word you want to locate.

3. Click the Options button and specify any desired options:

   - **Within:** Search just the current worksheet or the entire workbook.

   - **Search:** Select whether to search across the rows first, or down the columns first.

   - **Look In:** Select whether you want to search through the values or formula results, through the actual formulas, or look in the comments.

      Select Formulas when you are looking for a formula that references a specific cell address.

   - **Match Case:** Decide if you want your search to be case specific.

   - **Match Entire Cell Contents:** Decide if you want your search results to list only the items that exactly match your search criteria.

4. Click the Find Next button. Excel jumps to the first occurrence of the match (see Figure 8-12). If this is not the entry you are looking for, click the Find Next button again. Excel advises you if it does not locate the data you are searching for.

5. Click the Close button when you have located the entry you want.

Figure 8-11: The Find and Replace dialog box

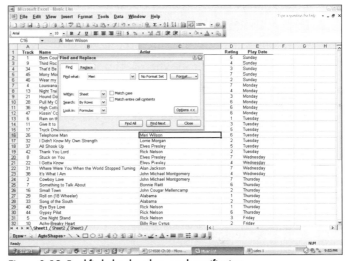

Figure 8-12: Excel finds data based on search specifications

Find All Data Occurrences

1. Choose Edit➪Find. In the Find What box, enter the value or word to locate.

2. Click the Options button and specify any desired options.

3. Click the Find All button. The Find and Replace dialog box expands showing a list of each cell entry that contains your data (see Figure 8-13).

4. Click any entry. The specified cell is selected.

5. Click the Close button when you finish.

Locate Cells Based on Format

1. Choose Edit➪Find. Click the Options button. Verify the options you want to use.

2. Click the Format button. The Find Format dialog box, shown in Figure 8-14, appears.

3. Select any formatting options on which you want to search. A preview appears in the Preview box. Click OK.

 Optionally, click the Choose Format from Cell button and select a cell already containing the formatting you want to search.

4. In the Find What box, enter the value or word you want to locate. Leave this blank if you want to locate only cells with the specified formatting, regardless of the cell contents.

5. Click the Find or the Find All button.

6. Click the Close button when finished.

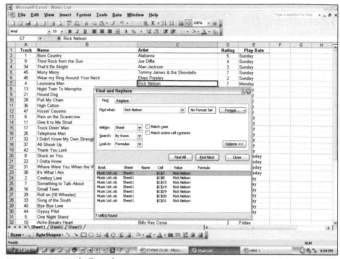

Figure 8-13: Find All results

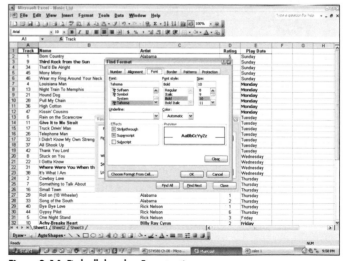

Figure 8-14: Find cells based on Format options

Use the Replace Command

1. Choose Edit⇨Replace (or press Ctrl+H). The Find and Replace dialog box opens with the Replace tab on top. (See Figure 8-15.)

    If you want to replace only data in certain cells, rows, or columns, select the desired area before you open the Find and Replace dialog box.

2. In the Find What box, enter the data you want to locate.

    Click the Options button to select additional search preferences. click the Format button and match the formatting you are searching for.

3. In the Replace With box, enter the data with which you want to replace the found data.

    Like the Find data, you can specify the replacement data have specific formatting.

4. Choose the Find Next button to locate the first found occasion or choose the Find All button to display a list of all occurrences.

5. If you want to use the replacement data, click the Replace button. Excel performs the replacement and locates the next occurrence.

6. If you want to replace all occurrences at the same time, choose the Replace All button. Excel displays an information box, shown in Figure 8-16, indicating the number of replacements made.

7. Click OK.

Figure 8-15: Exchange data with the Find and Replace feature

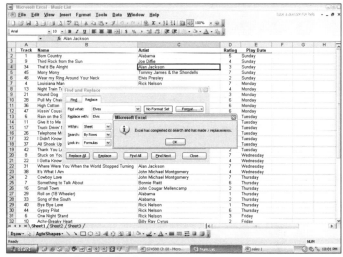

Figure 8-16: Making global replacements

Creating Charts with Excel

Chapter 9

*W*hoever said a picture is worth a thousand words is most certainly referring to a chart. Let's face it . . . we like looking at pictures more than we like looking at sheets of data. Charts, sometimes referred to as *graphs*, provide an effective way to illustrate your worksheet data by making the relationship between numbers easier to see because it turns numbers into shapes, and then the shapes can be compared to each other.

If you've ever spent hours drawing a chart on graph paper, you'll really appreciate the ease with which you can create dozens of different chart styles using your Excel data and you don't really have to draw a thing! With just a few decisions on your part, and a few clicks of the mouse, you have a two- or three-dimensional illustration of your data.

Charts let you get across your thoughts with simplicity and strength and because different charts draw you to different conclusions, they prod you to ask different questions about what you are seeing. Whatever the idea you are trying to convey, charts make it easier.

In this chapter, discover how to

- ➡ Quickly and easily create a chart
- ➡ Modify a chart whether in appearance or content
- ➡ Work with a 3-dimensional chart
- ➡ Design and create an organization chart

Get ready to. . .

Create a Basic Chart

1. Select the data (sequential or nonsequential) you want to plot in the chart. See Figure 9-1 for an example of sequential data selected for a chart.

2. Press the F11 key. Excel immediately adds a new sheet called Chart1 to your workbook with the data plotted into a column chart. Each subsequent chart page is numbered sequentially such as Chart2, Chart3, and so forth. Looking at Figure 9-2, you can see the various elements that make up a chart:

 Some newer keyboards use a different function for the F11 key. If your F11 key does not produce a chart, use the Excel Chart Wizard as explained in the next section.

 Throughout this chapter you find out how to edit the look and style of a chart, including creating a chart using the Excel Chart Wizard.

- **Title:** A descriptive name for the overall chart. By default, titles are not added in a basic chart, but you can add them later manually or by using the Chart Wizard.

- **X or Category axis:** Column or row headings from your selected data, which Excel uses for Category axis names. In a column chart, the categories display along the bottom. In other charts (such as a bar chart), the category axis displays along the left side.

- **Category label:** A descriptive name for the Category axis. By default, a category label is not added in a basic chart, but you can add one later manually or with the Chart Wizard.

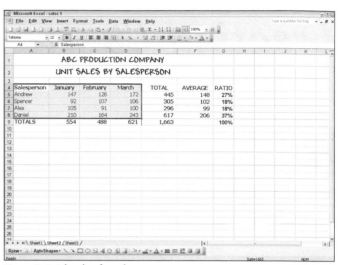

Figure 9-1: Select data for a chart

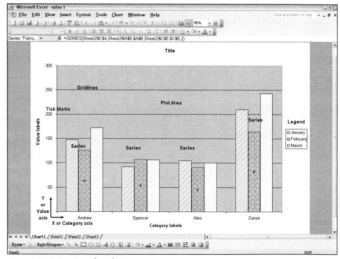

Figure 9-2: Viewing chart basics

- **Y or Value axis:** A scale representing the zero or the lowest and highest numbers in the plotted data. The Value axis is usually located on the left side on a column chart or on the bottom on a bar chart.

- **Value label:** A descriptive name for the values. By default, a value label is not added in a basic chart, but you can add one later manually or by using the Chart Wizard.

- **Legend:** The box, usually located on the right, identifies the patterns or colors that are assigned to the chart data series. Notice in Figure 9-3 how the legend explains that the striped series represents January, the checked series is for February, and the solid color series is for March.

- **Tick marks:** The small extension of lines that appear outside of the gray area and represent divisions of the value or category axis.

- **Gridlines:** These lines extend from the tick marks across the chart area, which allows you to easily view and evaluate data.

- **Series:** Excel uses the worksheet cell values to generate the series. Each element, called *data markers*, represents a single worksheet cell value and related data markers make up a data series and have the same pattern or color. In Figure 9-4, you can see the comparison of the data values to the y-axis and the series values.

- **Plot area:** The gray background that represents the entire plotted chart area.

 To delete this chart, right-click the Chart tab and choose Delete. When Excel asks for a confirmation, click Delete again.

 Use any of the drawing tools on the Drawing toolbar to annotate your chart such as adding arrows, circles, or text boxes. See Chapter 5 for more info.

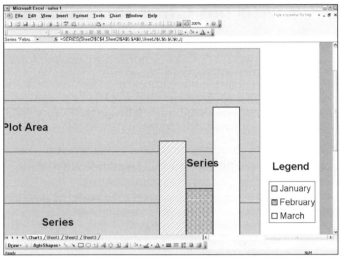

Figure 9-3: A chart legend

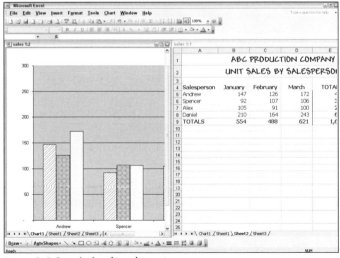

Figure 9-4: Data displayed in a data series

Work with the Chart Wizard

1. Select the data you want to plot in the chart. If you are selecting values such as monthly figures, you don't want to include totals in your chart.

2. Choose Insert➪Chart or click the Chart Wizard button on the Standard toolbar. The first screen of the Chart Wizard appears. (See Figure 9-5.)

3. Select the chart type you want to use (click a chart type to see a sample and an explanation of the chart):

   - **Column:** Column charts compare values to categories using a series of vertical columns to illustrate the series.

   - **Bar:** Bar charts, like column charts, compare values to categories, but use a series of horizontal bars to illustrate the series.

   - **Line:** Line charts are similar to bar charts but use dots to represent the data points and lines to connect the data points.

   - **Pie:** This chart compares parts to a whole. Usually a pie chart has only one data series (see Figure 9-6).

   - **Area:** Area charts display the trend of each value, usually over a specified period of time.

   - **X-Y Scatter:** These charts include two value axes, showing one set of numerical data along the x-axis and another along the y-axis.

   - **Surface:** Shows trends in values in a continuous curve.

   - **Doughnut:** Displays data similarly to a pie chart; it compares parts to a whole, but contains multiple series.

   - **Radar:** Displays changes in values relative to a center point by comparing the cumulative values of multiple data series.

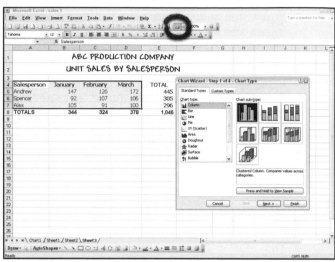

Figure 9-5: Screen 1 of the Chart Wizard

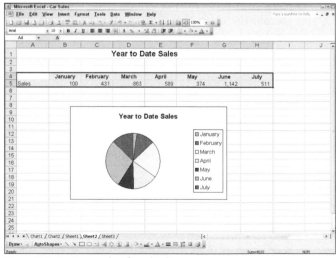

Figure 9-6: Create a pie chart from this data

- **Stock:** Stock charts (see Figure 9-7) illustrate the fluctuation of stock prices. In a stock chart, the data order is very important and usually the row headings are High, Low, and Close; or Open, High, Low, and Close.

- **Bubble:** These charts are similar to scatter charts, but compare three sets of values by displaying a series of circles.

- **Cylinder, Cone, and Pyramid:** These three charts create a column or bar chart using 3-dimensional shapes.

4. Choose a chart subtype. Depending on the chart type, some chart subtypes show the data series next to each other, others show the data stacked on top of each other. Additionally, some charts are 2-dimensional and others are 3-dimensional.

 If you are not sure which chart subtype is best for your data, click the Press and Hold to View Sample button to see your selected data in any chart style and subtype.

5. Click Next. Step 2 of Chart Wizard (shown in Figure 9-8) appears.

6. Select whether you want Excel to plot the data series from your columns of selected data or from the rows of selected data.

 To select different data for your chart, either type the correct cell address range in the Data Range text box, or click the spreadsheet icon at the end of the Data Range text box, highlight the desired data, and press Enter to return to the Chart Wizard.

7. Click Next. Step 3 of the Chart Wizard appears. The options you see depend on the chart type you selected.

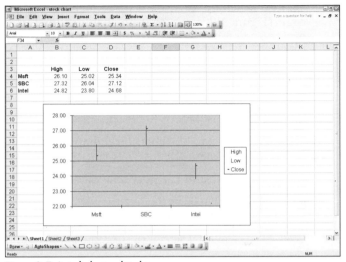

Figure 9-7: A stock chart and its data

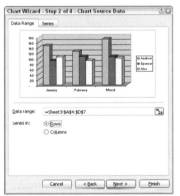

Figure 9-8: Screen 2 of the Chart Wizard

8. Choose which options you want to include with your chart (Figure 9-9 shows column chart options). The options you see depend on the chart type you selected:

   - **Titles:** Adds descriptive information to the chart and optionally to the category and value axes.

   - **Axes:** Displays or hides the primary axes of your chart.

   - **Gridlines:** Displays or hides chart gridlines.

   - **Legend:** Displays the chart legend and determines legend placement.

   - **Data Labels:** Adds category and value labels.

   - **Data Table:** Displays data values. See the "Add a Data Table" section.

9. Click Next. The final screen of the Chart Wizard appears.

10. Select whether you want Excel to place the chart on its own worksheet or whether you want it placed on the worksheet where your data resides.

11. Click the Finish button to create your chart.

 If you opt to place the chart on the existing worksheet, Excel treats it as a graphic image. Chapter 5 covers how to resize, move, or delete the chart.

Change the Chart Type

1. If the chart is on a regular worksheet, click the chart to select it. If it is on its own sheet, display the sheet. The menu changes to reflect the chart options.

2. Choose Chart⇨Chart Type. Select the chart type and subtype you want. (See Figure 9-10.)

3. Click OK. Excel modifies the existing chart.

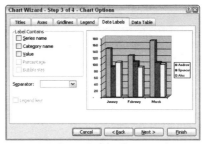

Figure 9-9: Screen 3 of the Chart Wizard

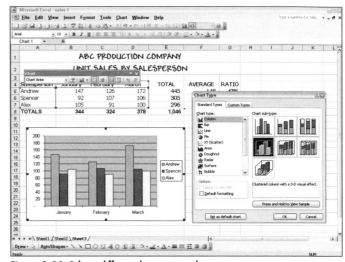

Figure 9-10: Select a different chart type or subtype

Include Titles and Labels

1. If you want to add a title to your chart, choose Chart⇨ Chart Options. The Chart Options dialog box opens, with the Titles tab showing (see Figure 9-11).

2. Enter a title in the Chart Title box.

3. Enter a name for the Category axis and the Value axis. Note that 3-dimensional charts may consider a z-axis for the value axis.

4. Click OK.

Customize the Chart Legend

1. To modify the Legend box (but not the series), select the Legend box.

2. Choose Format⇨Selected Legend. The Format Legend dialog box appears.

3. Click the Patterns tab and select the following options:

   • Color or fill effects for the background of the legend.

   • A border style that goes around the legend.

4. Click the Font tab and select a font, size, style, and color for the legend text. See Figure 9-12.

5. Click the Placement tab and select the legend location.

 Optionally, in the chart itself, you can drag the legend to any desired location.

6. Click OK. Excel makes the legend changes.

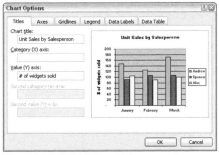

Figure 9-11: Add labels and titles to your chart

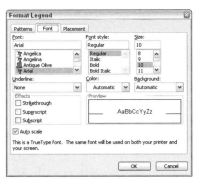

Figure 9-12: Modify the chart legend

Modify Chart Attributes

1. Double-click the chart element you want to modify. For example, if you want to change the style of the gridlines, double-click a gridline. If you want to apply different colors or patterns to a series, double-click any part that represents the series you want to change. The appropriate Format dialog box appears (Figure 9-13 shows the Format Data Series dialog box).

2. Make any desired changes in the Format dialog box.

    Click the Fill Effects button in the Format Data Series dialog box to add texture, gradients, or patterns to the series.

3. Click OK.

Add Graphic Images to a Series

1. Double-click the series you want to add an image to. The Format Data Series dialog box appears.

2. Click the Fill Effects button on the Patterns tab. The Fill Effects dialog box opens.

3. Click the Select Picture button on the Picture tab. The Select Picture dialog box opens.

4. Locate and select the picture you want to use.

5. Click the Insert button.

6. In the From the Format section of the Fill Effects dialog box, choose Stack.

7. Click OK twice. Figure 9-14 illustrates a bar chart where I changed one bar series to a graphic image.

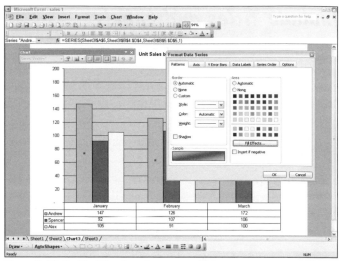

Figure 9-13: Double-click a chart element to modify it

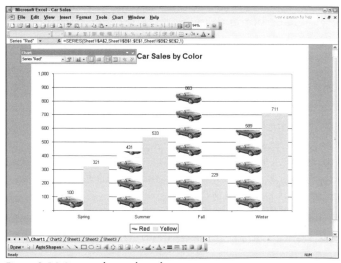

Figure 9-14: Liven up charts with graphic images

Change a Chart Location

1. Choose Chart⇨Chart Location. The Chart Location dialog box, shown in Figure 9-15, appears.

2. Select a location.

3. Click OK. Your chart is moved to the location you've specified.

Add a Data Table

1. To display a chart data table, click the sheet containing the chart.

You can add data tables to charts included with a regular worksheet, but it isn't a common practice because the worksheet itself already displays the data.

Data tables display the chart values in a grid beneath the chart. You'll find them very helpful if a reader needs to see exact values along with a graphical display, such as when using a 3-D chart.

2. Choose Chart⇨Chart Options.

3. Select the Data Table tab.

Data tables are not available for pie, scatter, bubble, radar, or surface chart types.

4. Select the Show Data Table option.

Be sure to check the Show Legend Keys box if you want the data table to display each legend next to the series label in the data table.

5. Click OK. A data table, as shown in Figure 9-16, displays at the bottom of the chart showing the actual values.

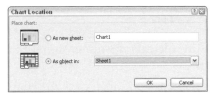

Figure 9-15: Switch a chart from one location to the other

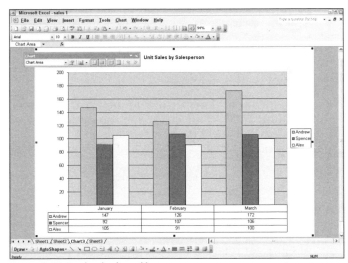

Figure 9-16: Display the data table

Enhance a 3-D Chart

1. Using the Chart Wizard, create a 3-dimensional chart. (See the "Work with the Chart Wizard" section.)

2. If the chart is on a regular worksheet, click the chart to select it. If it is on its own sheet, display the sheet.

     Just in case you don't like your changes, make sure to save your worksheet, which also saves your chart, before modifying chart attributes.

3. Choose Chart⇨3-D View. The 3-D View dialog box, shown in Figure 9-17, appears. The options you see depend on the chart type.

4. Click the up or down arrows to modify the up/down elevation angle of the chart. You can optionally type the elevation angle (between 10 and 80) in the Elevation text box.

     Click the Apply button to see the changes before you close the 3-D View box.

5. Click the left or right rotation arrows or enter the degree of left/right rotation (between 0 and 360) you want for the chart in the Rotation box.

6. Change the thickness of the bars or height of pie slices by entering a value (between 5 and 500) in the Height box.

7. Click OK. The chart appears on-screen, rotated to the angles you selected. Figure 9-18 shows a 3-D pie chart before and after changing the elevation, rotation, and depth. The pie also has a piece pulled out for emphasis.

Figure 9-17: Rotate a 3-dimensional chart

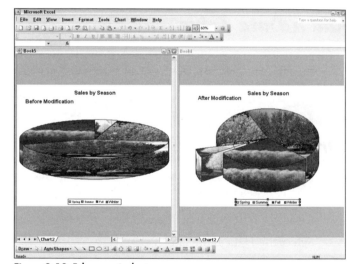

Figure 9-18: Enhance a pie chart

Add or Delete Data

1. To add or delete a series to a chart, choose Chart⇨ Source Data. The Source Data dialog box opens.

2. Alter the table data as you need:

   • **Add a series:** Click the Data Range tab, which displays the current chart data selected in the worksheet (see Figure 9-19). Use the mouse to select the new complete data range, including both the current data and the new data.

   • **Remove a series:** Click the Series tab. In the Series section, select the series name you want to remove and click the Remove button.

3. Click OK. The Source Data dialog box closes.

Format the Value Axis

1. Double-click the value axis, which displays the Format Axis dialog box.

2. Choose the options you want to change:

   • **Patterns:** Change the line styles used by the value axis.

   • **Scale:** Change a range by entering the maximum and minimum values, as shown in Figure 9-20.

   • **Font:** Change the value font name, size, and appearance.

   • **Number:** Format the range as currency, including decimal points and dollar signs.

   • **Alignment:** Change the value orientation. This option is rarely used.

3. Click OK when you're done.

Figure 9-19: Add additional data values to the chart

Figure 9-20: Change the value scale

Create an Organization Chart

1. Choose Insert⇨Picture⇨Organizational Chart. A sample organization chart like the one in Figure 9-21 appears on the current worksheet along with an Organization Chart toolbar.

2. Click a box and type a name or position. Press Enter to add a second line if desired and apply any formatting.

    Double-click any box to change the individual box background color.

3. Using the Organization Chart toolbar, make other chart layout changes as follows (Figure 9-22 shows a modified org chart):

   • **Add additional subordinates, coworkers, or assistant**: Click the box to which you want to add a subordinate, coworker, or assistant. Select the appropriate choice from the Insert Shape drop-down list. A new box appears under or next to the previously selected box.

   • **Change the overall layout**: Select a different layout from the Layout drop-down list.

   • **Change the connecting line styles:** Choose All Connecting Lines from the Select drop-down list. Double-click any line and change the style in the Format AutoShape box. Click OK.

    Other charts not based on Excel values (called *diagrams*) include Cycle, Radial, Pyramid, Venn, and Target. Choose Insert⇨Diagram, select the type of diagram you want, and then click OK. Use the Diagram toolbar to annotate or edit the diagram.

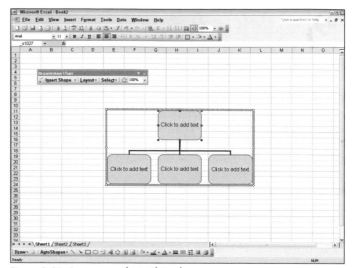

Figure 9-21: Create an org chart with Excel

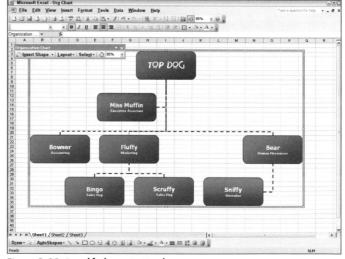

Figure 9-22: A modified organization chart

Printing Workbooks

*W*hen you finish compiling your worksheet, you'll probably want to print a hard copy or e-mail a copy to someone else. This chapter shows you a number of Excel tools you can use to improve your document layout, including headers, footers, page orientation, and margins.

Also, before you print or give your Excel file to someone else, you should check it for spelling errors because typos can stand out screaming "I can't spell." Excel includes a built-in dictionary you can use to check your workbooks for misspellings; however, it can't read your mind, so if you type *too* instead of *two*, Excel probably won't indicate that as an error. But, combine the spell check with proofreading on your part, and you'll find a very helpful tool.

When printing, Excel assumes you want to print the entire worksheet area unless you specify otherwise. You discover how to specify exactly what you want to print. This chapter also includes these topics:

- Working with page breaks
- Adjusting the paper size
- Making your worksheet fit better on a page for those times when you want to get that last few rows or columns on a single page
- Printing gridlines or row and column headings on the page as well as other print options that you might want to select when printing your worksheet or chart

Chapter 10

Get ready to. . .

Spell Check

1. Choose Tools⇨Spelling or click the Spelling icon on the Standard toolbar. The Spelling dialog box opens and Excel highlights the cell with the first potential misspelling along with suggested changes (as shown in Figure 10-1).

   Optionally, press F7 to start the spell check.

   Spell check reviews all cell values, comments, embedded charts, text boxes, buttons, and headers and footers, but it does not check protected worksheets, formulas, or text that results from a formula.

2. Select one of the following options:

   • **Change or Change All:** Choose one of the suggestions; then click Change to change just this incident of the spelling mistake or Change All if you think you could have made the mistake more than once.

   • **AutoCorrect:** Have Excel, in future workbooks, automatically correct the mistake with the selected replacement.

   • **Ignore Once:** Click this button if you don't want to change the highlighted instance of the spelling.

   • **Ignore All:** Click this button if you don't want to change any instances of the spelling.

   • **Add to Dictionary:** Add a word to Excel's built-in dictionary so that Excel won't flag it as a potential error in the future.

3. After you select an option, Excel proceeds to the next error, and when all potential mistakes are identified, click OK (as shown in Figure 10-2).

Figure 10-1: Use the spell check to correct errors

Figure 10-2: The completed spell check message box

Preview Before Printing

1. Choose File➪Print Preview or click the Print Preview icon on the Standard toolbar.

2. From the Print Preview screen (shown in Figure 10-3), select from the following options:

     I cover many of the Print Preview options in greater detail later in this chapter.

    - If there are multiple pages, click the Next or Previous buttons to view additional pages.

    - Click the Zoom button to enlarge the view. Click a second time to reduce the view.

    - Click the Print button to display the Print dialog box.

    - Click the Setup button to display the Page Setup dialog box.

    - Click the Margins button to display the page margins; then drag any margin line to manually set margin sizes. Click the Margins button again to turn off the margin lines.

    - Click the Page Break Preview button; then click OK to display the worksheet in Page Break Preview mode. You can manually adjust where the page breaks occur by dragging any blue page break line (see Figure 10-4). You can also resize the print area and edit the worksheet. Return to Normal view from Page Break Preview by choosing View➪Normal.

3. Click the Close button to return to Normal view.

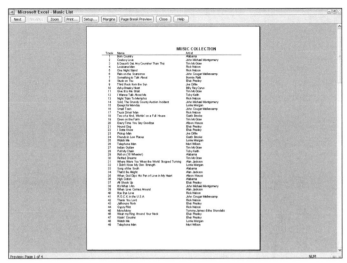

Figure 10-3: Print Preview options

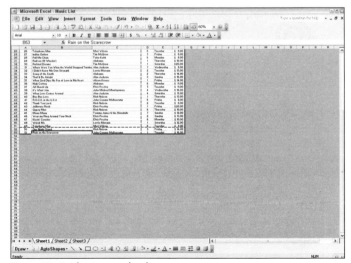

Figure 10-4: Adjusting page breaks

Add a Manual Page Break

1. Click a cell in the row where you want the new page to begin.

2. Choose Insert⇨Page Break. Dotted page break lines similar to the ones in Figure 10-5 appear.

 To remove the manual page break, click a cell in the row just below the page break and choose Insert⇨Remove Page Break.

 Optionally, adjust page breaks through Page Break Preview mode. Choose View⇨Page Break Preview.

Set a Specific Area to Print

1. Highlight the area you want to print. See Figure 10-6.

 Unless you specify a print area, Excel prints the entire worksheet.

2. Choose File⇨Print Area⇨Set Print Area. Dotted lines appear around the print area. When you print the worksheet, only the area within the boundaries print. See the "Print Worksheets or Charts" section, later in this chapter to print.

 To reset Excel to print the entire worksheet, choose File⇨Print Area⇨Clear Print Area.

 Optionally, highlight the area you want to print and from the Print dialog box, choose Selection in the Print What section.

Figure 10-5: Insert a manual page break

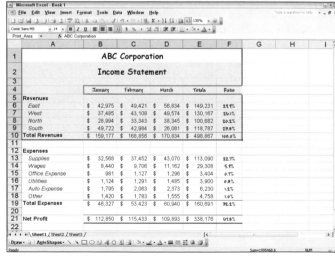

Figure 10-6: Specify a specific print area

Adjust the Paper Size and Orientation

1. Choose File⇨Page Setup. The Page Setup dialog box opens.

2. From the Page tab (see Figure 10-7), select whether you want a Portrait or Landscape orientation from the Orientation section. Portrait orientation prints the top along the short edge of the paper and Landscape prints along the long edge of the paper.

3. Select a paper size from the Paper Size drop-down list. The paper size choices you see depend on the printer you use. The two most common choices are Letter (which is 8.5 inches by 11 inches) and Legal (which is 8.5 inches by 14 inches).

4. Click OK.

Make Worksheets Fit Better on a Page

1. Choose File⇨Page Setup. The Page Setup dialog box opens.

2. Click the Page tab.

3. From the Scaling area, make a selection from the options shown in Figure 10-8:

   • **Adjust To:** Enlarge or shrink the printed font size by setting a percentage option between 10 and 400.

   • **Fit To:** Force Excel to a specified number of pages wide and tall.

 Don't try to shrink the document too much. Because Excel shrinks the font, trying to fit too much on a page can make the document too small to read.

4. Click OK.

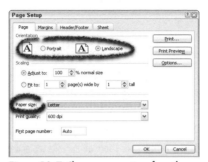

Figure 10-7: Choose paper options from the Page tab

Figure 10-8: Squeeze your worksheet onto a specified number of pages

Set Page Margins

1. Choose File➪Page Setup. The Page Setup dialog box opens.

2. Click the Margins tab (shown in Figure 10-9) and set the margins for the top, bottom, left, and right side of the page.

     The default worksheet margins are 1 inch on both the top and bottom and .75 inch on the left and right sides.

     Click the Horizontally and/or the Vertically options in the Center on Page section to center the worksheet on the page, regardless of the margins.

3. Click OK.

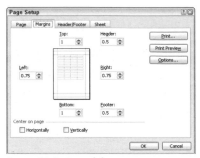

Figure 10-9: Set worksheet page margins

Add a Standard Header or Footer

1. Choose File➪Page Setup. The Page Setup dialog box opens.

2. Click the Header/Footer tab. See Figure 10-10.

     Headers appear at the top of each printed page and footers appear at the bottom of each printed page.

3. Select a header from the Header drop-down list.

4. Select a footer from the Footer drop-down list.

5. Click OK.

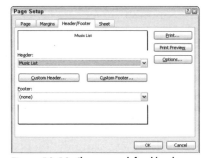

Figure 10-10: Choose a predefined header or footer

Create a Custom Header or Footer

1. Choose File⇨Page Setup. The Page Setup dialog box opens.

2. From the Header/Footer tab, click the Custom Header (or Custom Footer) button. The Header (or Footer) dialog box appears (see Figure 10-11).

3. In any desired section, type the text you want for the header (or footer).

4. Select any text and click the Font button to select font options.

5. Optionally, click one of the other buttons to insert date or file codes:

   • **Page:** Insert a code that indicates the page number.

   • **Pages:** Insert a code that indicates the total number of pages.

    You can add text to the Page text. For example: `Page &[Page] of &[Pages]` prints `Page 3 of 5` or `Page 1 of 2`.

   • **Date or Time:** Insert the print date or time of day (see Figure 10-12).

   • **Path, File Name, or Sheet Tab Name:** Include file information.

   • **Insert Picture:** Insert a graphic image such as a company logo.

   • **Format Picture:** Resize, rotate, or crop a header or footer graphic image.

6. Click OK.

Figure 10-11: Add your own text to a header or footer

Figure 10-12: Insert the print date in the header or footer

Specify Repeating Rows and Columns

1. Choose File⇨Page Setup. The Page Setup dialog box opens.

2. Click the Sheet tab. Type a dollar sign ($) followed by the row numbers or column letters you want to print as titles in the Print Titles section. Entering **$1:$2**, as you see in Figure 10-13, repeats rows 1 and 2 at the beginning of each page.

Click the worksheet icon on the right to collapse the Page Setup dialog box so you can select the rows or columns you want to include. Click the button again to return to the Page Setup dialog box.

3. Click OK.

Print Gridlines and Column Headings

1. Choose File⇨Page Setup.

2. Click the Sheet tab. In the Print section, choose the following options:

   • **Gridlines:** Print the gridlines surrounding each cell in the worksheet.

   • **Row and Column Headings:** Print the row numbers or column letters around the worksheet.

3. Click OK. Figure 10-14 illustrates a worksheet printed with gridlines and row and column headings.

By default, gridlines are a lighter shade of gray. You can change the gridline color by choosing Tools⇨Options and selecting a gridline color from the View tab.

Figure 10-13: Select rows or columns to repeat at the top of each page

Figure 10-14: A printed worksheet with column and row headings and gridlines

Print Worksheets and Charts

1. Choose File⇨Print. The Print dialog box, shown in Figure 10-15 appears.

 Optionally, print the worksheet immediately by clicking the Print button on the Standard toolbar.

2. Choose from the following options:

- **Name:** Select a printer different than the default printer.

- **Print Range:** Specify whether to print the entire worksheet as determined by the print area, or whether to print only specific pages.

- **Copies:** Select the number of copies you want to print.

- **Print What:** Choose whether to print the current worksheet, a preselected area, or the entire workbook.

3. Click OK.

E-Mail a Workbook

1. Choose File⇨Send To⇨Mail Recipient (as Attachment). As you see in Figure 10-16, your e-mail program launches with the worksheet as an attachment.

 Recipients must have Excel installed on their systems to open the workbook file. If they don't have Excel, send the worksheet as the body of the e-mail instead of an attachment by choosing File⇨ Send To⇨Mail Recipient.

2. Enter the recipient e-mail information and enter any additional text in the body of the message.

3. Click the Send button.

Figure 10-15: Select from a plethora of print options

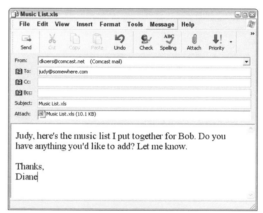

Figure 10-16: E-mail Excel information to others

Part IV
Analyzing Data with Excel

The 5th Wave   By Rich Tennant

"Somebody got through our dead end Web links, past the firewalls, and around the phone prompt loops. Before you know it, the kid here picks up the phone and he's talking one on one to a customer."

Working with Outlines

*Y*ou can use Excel to automatically calculate subtotal and grand total values from rows containing related data (sometimes called a *database*). When you create subtotals, Excel outlines the list so that you can display and hide the detail rows for each subtotal.

Before you use the subtotal function, you must first sort your list so that the rows you want to subtotal are grouped together. You can then calculate subtotals and other mathematical calculations for any column that contains numbers, or you can count the number of items in a selected field.

If your data is not in a database format, you can still group sections together, allowing you a quick way to display or hide the sections as needed. Similar to using subtotals, Excel displays groups in an outline format. In this chapter, I take a look at the extensive subtotaling, grouping, and outlining features contained in Excel.

Chapter

11

Get ready to . . .

Generate a Subtotal

1. Sort the field by which you want to generate subtotals.

    The subtotal data must have no blank rows or columns, and each column in the database must have a label in the first row.

2. Choose Data➪Subtotals. The Subtotal dialog box appears.

3. Select the field you want to subtotal from the At Each Change In drop-down list.

4. Select a function from the Use Function drop-down list. Choices include SUM (totals the values in a field), COUNT (returns the quantity of items in a field), AVERAGE (determines the average value of a field), MAX and MIN (display the highest and lowest value in a field), and PRODUCT (returns the value of all the numbers in a field multiplied together).

5. Select the fields you want to subtotal from the Add Subtotal To drop-down list. (See Figure 11-1.) You can select more than one field to subtotal.

6. Check the Replace Current Subtotals box if you already have a previous subtotal calculation. Excel replaces the previous subtotals with the new one.

7. Check the Page Break Between Groups box if you want Excel to begin each subtotaled group on a new page.

8. Remove the check from the Summary Below Data box if you want Excel to place the subtotals at the top of each group instead of under each group.

9. Click OK. Excel performs the subtotal. Figure 11-2 shows sales subtotaled by Sales Rep.

Figure 11-1: Select fields to calculate

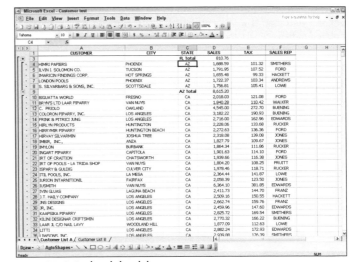

Figure 11-2: A subtotaled worksheet

Collapse Subtotal Headings

1. Create subtotals of your data. (See the preceding "Generate a Subtotal" section.)

 With subtotals, Excel defines groups in the form of an outline and bases the groups on the rows used to calculate the subtotals.

2. Hide and show data as you need with the following methods (see Figure 11-3):

   - **See only the grand total.** Click the 1 on the subtotal headings.

   - **See the subtotal categories and amounts (the detail is hidden).** Click the 2 on the subtotal headings (the column on the left side of the worksheet).

   - **Show all the detail and subtotals:** Click the 3 on the subtotal headings. Excel displays the individual worksheet rows.

Control Individual Subtotals

1. Create subtotals for your data (see the "Generate a Subtotal" section, earlier in this chapter).

2. Click the Hide Detail button (minus sign) next to any subtotal row. As seen in Figure 11-4, the selected subtotal detail collapses. It's not lost, only hidden.

3. Click the Show Detail button (plus sign) next to any subtotal row. The detail data for the selected row appears.

 Optionally, choose Data➪Group and Outline➪Hide Detail or Show Detail.

Figure 11-3: Collapse and expand entire subtotal sections

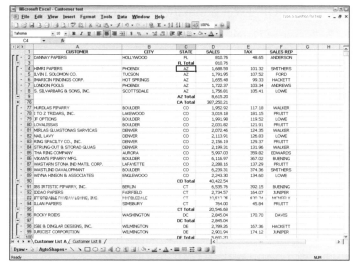

Figure 11-4: Collapse and expand individual sections

Create Multiple Subtotals

1. From the Sort dialog box, select the column by which you want to generate primary subtotals and the column by which you want to generate secondary subtotals. For example, if you want to first subtotal sales by state and then by city, you would also sort first by state and then by city.

2. Choose Data⇨Subtotals to display the Subtotals dialog box.

3. Select the primary field you want to subtotal from the At Each Change drop-down list. Figure 11-5 shows the primary field as the State field.

4. Select a function from the Use Function drop-down list.

5. Select the fields you want to subtotal from the Add Subtotal To drop-down list.

6. Click OK. Excel summarizes the data by the selected field.

7. Choose Data⇨Sort. Excel again displays the Sort dialog box.

8. Select the secondary field you want to subtotal, the type of function, and the fields you want to subtotal. In my example, I use the City field.

9. Deselect the Replace Current Subtotals box.

10. Click OK. Figure 11-6 illustrates both the sales amount and the sales tax subtotaled by state and then by city.

 As you perform additional subtotaling, Excel adds additional levels. In Figure 11-6, four heading levels are displayed. Level 1 displays only the grand totals, level 2 displays the totals by state, level 3 shows the totals by city and state, and level 4 displays the detail.

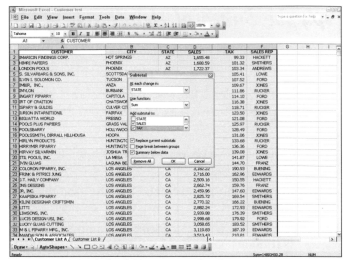

Figure 11-5: Select the first field you want to subtotal

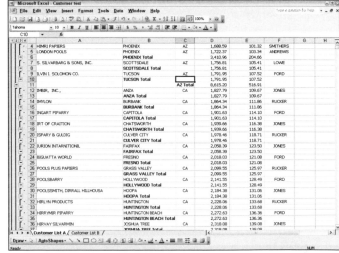

Figure 11-6: Click the heading levels to expand or collapse the subtotals

Copy Subtotals

1. Hide any unwanted Detail button by clicking the Expand or Collapse buttons.

2. Select the data you want to copy.

3. Choose Edit⇨Go To, which displays the Go To dialog box.

4. Click the Special button. The Go To Special dialog box opens (see Figure 11-7).

5. Select the Visible Cells Only option. White lines appear around the selected cells.

 Another use for the Go To Special dialog box is if you want to select only cells with constant values or to select only cells containing formulas.

6. Click OK.

7. Choose Edit⇨Copy (or press Ctrl+C). A marquee appears around the selected cells.

8. Select the beginning cell where you want to place the copied data.

9. Choose Edit⇨Paste (or press Ctrl+V). Excel duplicates only the subtotaled values, not the formulas or hidden cells.

Remove Subtotals

1. Choose Data⇨Subtotals. The Subtotal dialog box opens (see Figure 11-8).

2. Click the Remove All button. Excel removes all subtotal information from the database.

Figure 11-7: The Go To Special dialog box

Figure 11-8: Remove subtotals from the database

Use AutoOutline

1. Choose Data➪Group and Outline➪AutoOutline.
Figure 11-9 illustrates a worksheet with outline headings for both rows and columns. Row outline symbols are on the left, and column outline symbols are at the top of the worksheet.

 AutoOutline works best if the worksheet has summary formulas that reference cells in the detail cells. The summary formulas must be adjacent to the detail.

 AutoOutline assumes your summary rows are below the detail rows or to the right of the detail columns. If your worksheet summary rows are above or to the left of the detail, choose Data➪Group and Outline➪Settings and uncheck the Summary Rows Below Detail check box and/or the Summary Columns to Right of Detail option.

 You can create and apply styles to an outline, or you can apply AutoFormats to an outline. You can apply the formatting either before or after you create the outline. See Chapter 4. To apply an automatic style, choose Data➪Group and Outline➪Settings and select the Automatic Styles check box.

2. To expand the outline, click the Show Detail buttons to the left of the rows or above the column headings. (See Figure 11-10.)

3. To collapse the outline, click the Hide buttons to the left of the rows or above the column headings.

4. To remove the AutoOutline, choose Data➪Group and Outline➪Clear Outline.

 To hide an outline without removing it, display all the data by clicking the highest number in the outline symbols and then choosing Tools➪ Options. Click the View tab and clear the Outline Symbols check box.

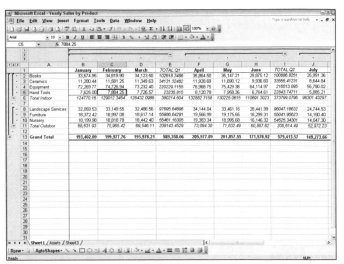

Figure 11-9: A worksheet with outline headings

Figure 11-10: Click the plus or minus buttons to hide or display parts of the workbook

Form an Outline Group

1. Highlight the rows or columns that you want to group together.

2. Choose Data➪Group and Outline➪Group. In Figure 11-11, you see where all the vehicles in the asset list are grouped together.

   Click the Hide or Show Detail buttons to hide or display the group detail.

3. Repeat Steps 1 and 2 until you have created all the levels you want in the outline.

Remove Items from a Group

1. Select the rows or columns you want to remove from the group. If you want to remove an entire group, select all the rows or columns in the group.

2. Choose Data➪Group and Outline➪Ungroup. Excel removes the rows or columns from the group and if the rows or columns you delete are in the middle of a group, Excel breaks the group into two smaller groups. See Figure 11-12, where the vehicles are broken from one group into two smaller groups.

   Optionally, ungroup sections by holding the Shift key, clicking the Hide or Display buttons, and then choosing Data➪Group and Outline➪Ungroup. Excel does not delete any data when you remove items from a group.

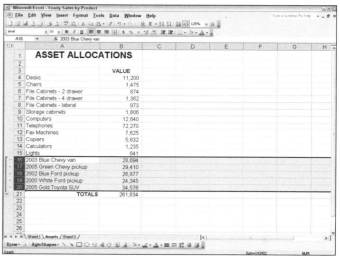

Figure 11-11: Create a manual group

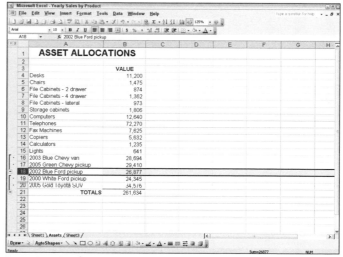

Figure 11-12: Splitting up groups

Filtering Data

*A*fter you create an Excel database and assemble a large amount of data, you'll probably want to analyze it. You may want to ask yourself questions about your data such as "Who are my best customers?", "Which inventory items are provided by a specific supplier and cost less than a certain amount?", or "Which employees work the least amount of hours?" Excel includes several tools you can use to study your data so you can make better decisions.

This chapter is about filtering, where Excel pulls out specific records for review, providing you an easy way to break your data into smaller more manageable chunks. Filtering does not rearrange your data; it simply temporarily hides records you don't want to review, so you can clearly examine those you do.

You can create your database by just typing in the Excel screen, or you can use an Excel data entry screen. In the first section, you see how to create a data entry screen for assistance in creating your database. But, remember, you don't have to use the data entry screen to use the filtering.

The remainder of the chapter is devoted to the different ways you can filter your data including

➡ Using AutoFilter, which allows you to select key pieces of data.

➡ Selecting records by more than one condition.

➡ Displaying only the top *x* number of records.

➡ Multiple filtering where you locate records that either match all criteria, or belong to one or the other criteria.

➡ Advanced filtering where you designate a specific area of your worksheet to manage your criteria selections.

Chapter 12

Get ready to. . .

Create a Data Entry Screen

1. Enter the column headings for your database. When you create the data entry screen, the column headings appear as field names.

    For faster data entry, format any numerical columns with the desired number format. Then, when you use the data entry screen, you need to enter only the raw numbers without commas or dollar signs.

2. Click in any heading cell; then choose Data⇨Form.

3. Click OK at the message box that appears. Excel displays a data form with the headings shown as field names (see Figure 12-1). Each label has a blank field to enter the data.

    If you already have data entered into your database, Excel does not display the message box.

    Using a data form makes data entry easier than typing across the columns when you have a wide range with more columns than can fit on the screen at one time.

4. Enter the first record information, pressing the Tab key to move from field to field (see Figure 12-2).

    Press Shift+Tab key to move back to the previous field.

5. Click the New button. Excel adds the record to the database and displays another blank screen ready for the next record.

6. Click Close when you finish entering data. Reopen the database form at any time by choosing Data⇨Form.

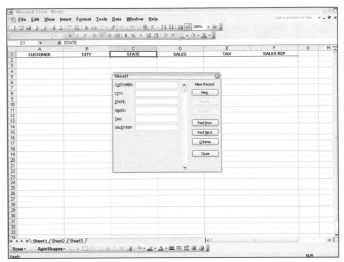

Figure 12-1: Create a data form

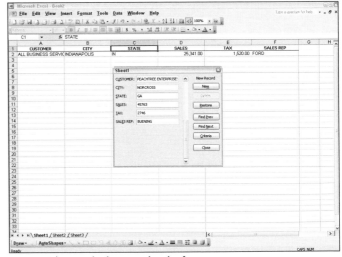

Figure 12-2: Enter database records with a form

Filter Data with AutoFilter

1. After clicking anywhere in your database, choose Data⇨Filter⇨AutoFilter. Excel displays an arrow in each database column.

2. Click the arrow in the column heading. Excel displays a drop-down list, which includes one of each unique entry (up to 1000 entries) in the selected column. See Figure 12-3. Besides the option of finding an exact match, the choices include

   - **Top 10:** Displays the 10 most (or least) repeated items. See the "Select Only the Top 10" section.

   - **Custom:** Prompts you to customize the filter. See the "Customize an AutoFilter" section.

   - **Blanks:** Displays all records with a blank in the selected field.

   - **NonBlanks:** Displays all records with data in the selected field. This hides the blank records.

   - **All:** Redisplays the entire list.

   Press Alt+Down Arrow while in any column to display the AutoFilter list for the current column.

3. Click the entry you want to filter. Excel displays only the records that match your choice. In Figure 12-4, for example, you see only the customers from Cincinnati.

4. Choose Data⇨Filter⇨Show All to redisplay all entries.

   Optionally, click the AutoFilter arrow from the filtered column and choose (All).

5. When you finish filtering your data, choose Data⇨Filter⇨AutoFilter to turn off the AutoFilter.

Figure 12-3: AutoFilter selections

Figure 12-4: Filter by city

Perform a Secondary Filter Selection

1. Turn on the AutoFilter by choosing Data⇨Filter⇨ AutoFilter.

2. Click the column arrow by which you want to first filter data.

3. Choose the data you want to filter. In Figure 12-5, you see selections only containing the city of Atlanta. However, notice that there is an Atlanta in GA, IN, and SC.

4. To further isolate specific items, click the AutoFilter arrow at the top of another column.

5. Select the field by which you want to perform the second filter. In Figure 12-6, the primary option was by the city of Atlanta, but I apply the state of GA to the secondary filter.

6. Repeat Steps 4 and 5 to further filter by additional fields as many times as you need.

7. When you're done looking at your filtered data, choose one of these options:

   • **Return to the first filter:** Click the second filter column arrow and choose a different second filter.

   • **Return to the first filter only:** Click the second filter column arrow and choose Show All.

   • **Return to viewing all records:** Choose Data⇨Filter⇨ Show All.

 Optionally, click the AutoFilter arrow from the filtered column and choose (All).

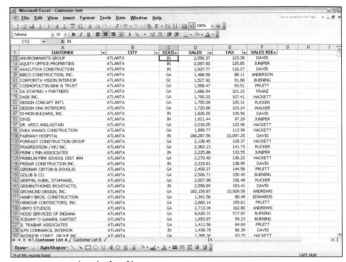

Figure 12-5: Select the first filter

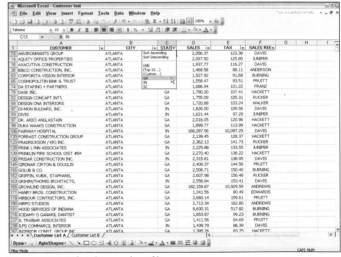

Figure 12-6: Select the second sort filter

Select Only the Top 10

1. Turn on the AutoFilter by choosing Data⫼Filter⫼ AutoFilter.

2. Click the column arrow by which you want to filter data. This column must contain numeric data.

3. Choose Top 10. The Top 10 AutoFilter dialog box appears, as shown in Figure 12-7.

Use the Top 10 AutoFilter to filter for the smallest or largest numbers.

4. From the first option, select whether you want the top (highest) or bottom (lowest) values.

5. In the second option, select the number of items you want to see (from 1 to 500).

6. In the third option, select whether you want to filter the items by their name or by their percentile. For example, choose to list the top 10 customers per their sales dollars, or list the top 10 percent of your customer base.

7. Click OK. In Figure 12-8, you see the top 10 customers by their sales values, sorted by record number.

To return to the filter options, click the current filter column arrow and choose a different filter.

Click a Sort button on the Standard toolbar to sort the records by their value.

8. When you're ready to view all records, choose Data⫼Filter⫼Show All.

Figure 12-7: The Top 10 AutoFilter dialog box

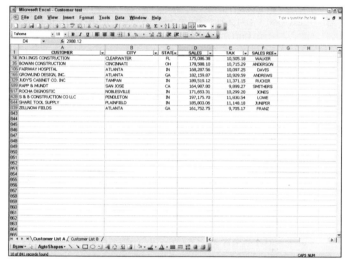

Figure 12-8: Selecting the top 10

Customize an AutoFilter

1. Turn on the AutoFilter by choosing Data➪Filter➪ AutoFilter.

2. Click the column arrow by which you want to first filter data.

3. Choose Custom. The Custom AutoFilter dialog box, shown in Figure 12-9, appears.

Figure 12-9: The Custom AutoFilter dialog box

 Use a Custom filter when you need to select a range of data instead of a single piece of data. For example, use the Custom filter when you want to find any value greater than a specified amount or where the data contain specific characters.

4. Select a qualifier from the first drop-down list (see Figure 12-10):

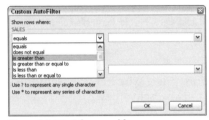

Figure 12-10: Select a qualifier

   - Equal To and Does Not Equal

   - Greater Than and Less Than

   - Greater Than Or Equal To and Less Than Or Equal To

   - Begins With and Does Not Begin With

   - Ends With and Does Not End With

   - Contains and Does Not Contain

 The qualifiers can apply to label or value cells.

5. Select a value to go with the qualifier from the second drop-down list or type a value in the text box.

6. Click OK. The filtered data now matches the data criteria.

Find Multiple Criteria

1. Turn on the AutoFilter by choosing Data⇨Filter⇨ AutoFilter.

2. Click the column arrow by which you want to first filter data.

3. Choose Custom. The Customize AutoFilter dialog box appears.

4. Select the first qualifier from the first drop-down list.

5. Select the second qualifier from the second drop-down list.

When using the AutoFilter, both qualifiers filter on the same field. For example, if the first qualifier filters on the Sales field, the second qualifier filters on the Sales field also. If you want to filter on two separate fields, such as Sales and State, then you must use the Advanced Filter. See the next section "Use Advanced Filtering."

6. Select a matching option:

- **And:** Your data must match both qualifications. In Figure 12-11, the Sales values must be greater than $50,000 and be less than $100,000. This allows the sale of $61,833.51 (D32), but the sale of $2,988.12 (D4) and $175,086.38 (D34) would not be included.

- **Or:** Your data must match only one of the two qualifications. For example, if the first qualifier specifies the sales value must be less than 50,000 or be greater than 100,000, then the sale of $2,988.12 in cell D4, and the one of $175,086.38 in D34 would be included in the filter, but the sale of $61,833.51 in D32 would not be included.

7. Click OK. In Figure 12-12, you see only records whose sales fall between the two values.

Figure 12-11: Select two qualifiers and a match option

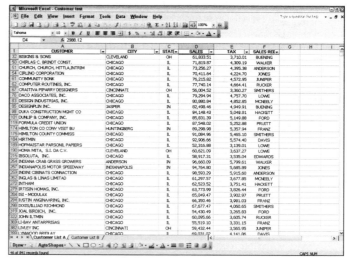

Figure 12-12: Matching multiple criteria

Use Advanced Filtering

1. Make sure the AutoFilter is turned off.

2. Select the first four rows of the worksheet.

3. Choose Insert⇨Rows, which inserts the blank rows at the top of your worksheet. Excel uses these as your criteria range.

    At least one blank row needs to separate your criteria range from your actual database. By inserting four rows, you are creating the opportunity to create three criteria options.

4. Select the header row of your database.

5. Choose Edit⇨Copy. A marquee appears.

6. Click the first cell of the first blank row.

7. Choose Edit⇨Paste to copy the header row of your database to the first blank row (Row 1). You now have a criteria range ready to enter filter selections (see Figure 12-13).

    While you could just retype the header row, using the copy and paste feature protects you against typing errors. The criteria area header row must exactly match the database header row.

8. In the first blank row of the criteria range, enter the data you want to match. For example, if you want to locate any entries for the state of California, type **California** under the State heading.

9. Enter any additional filter criteria:

   - **Create an And filter:** If you want Excel to find data that meets more than one restriction, enter the desired additional criteria in another field on the first criteria row.

   - **Create an Or filter:** Enter the filter data on the second row of the criteria range. See Figure 12-14 where I've added data to both the State and Sales columns.

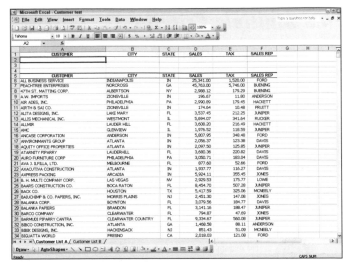

Figure 12-13: Insert blank rows for a criteria range

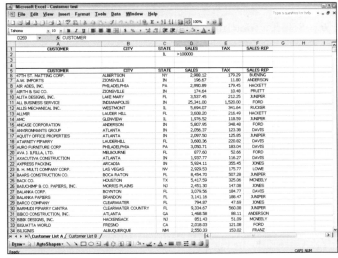

Figure 12-14: Enter your criteria

You can use Greater Than, Greater Than Or Equal To, Less Than, or Less Than Or Equal To as operators in your criteria range. For example, to find sales greater than or equal to 100, enter **>=100** in the Sales criteria row.

10. Click any cell in the main part of the database.

11. Choose Data⇨Filter⇨Advanced Filter. Excel displays the Advanced Filter dialog box.

12. Select the Filter the List, In Place option in the Action section.

13. Verify the database range in the List Range box.

14. Enter the criteria range. Excel provides two different ways:

- Type the criteria range including the header row, but not any blank rows. For example, in Figure 12-15, the criteria range is A1: F2.

Be sure to specify only the rows that contain filtering information. If you include blank rows in your criteria range, Excel includes it in the filtering with the effect of not filtering out any data, thereby returning all records.

- Click the Collapse button to the right of the Criteria Range box and highlight the entire criteria range, including the header row, but not any blank rows. Press Enter to return to the Advanced Filter dialog box.

15. Click OK. Excel places the results of your search in place of your original database (as shown in Figure 12-16).

You cannot place filtered data on a different sheet than the original data, but you can copy and paste it to a different sheet.

16. When you're ready to view all data records, choose Data⇨Filter⇨Show All.

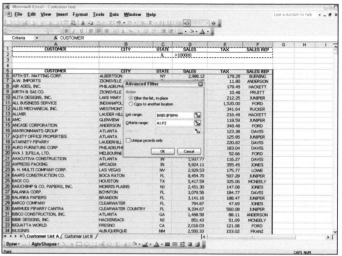

Figure 12-15: Enter the criteria range

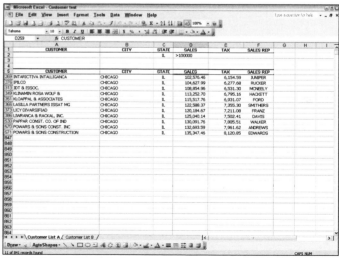

Figure 12-16: A filtered database

Creating Pivot Tables

Many people don't use PivotTables because they find them overwhelming. Yet, this powerful Excel tool helps you, within an instant, see your spreadsheet data in a variety of different ways. PivotTable reports allow you to group information, along with varying levels of detail, by different criteria, such as date or category. They automatically create subtotals of your data on a separate worksheet, which leaves your raw data untouched.

However, PivotTable calculations aren't limited to adding the numbers together. You can use Count, Average, Maximum, Minimum, and a number of other statistical functions to help you view the overall picture of your data.

You can fill any of the four main PivotTable areas with your data by a drag of the mouse and you can display the data in a table format or in one of Excel's many chart formats.

In this chapter, you find out how you can, within a matter of seconds, generate and extract meaningful information from a large amount of data, thereby saving you potentially dozens of hours of manual calculations.

Get ready to. . .

Create a PivotTable

1. Organize your data in a list, while keeping these points in mind:

    - Each column should contain only one type of data, such as dates in one column and values in another column.

    - Make sure each column in the list has a heading label directly above the data. (See Figure 13-1 for an example.) PivotTables use the column headings as PivotTable fields.

    - Do not leave any blank rows between the data and the row headings and no blank columns within the data.

    - Avoid blank cells within the data. If you have duplicate data, use the Copy command to replicate it in the blank cells.

    - If you have more than one list on the same worksheet, make sure at least one blank column and one blank row separate them. Figure 13-2 illustrates a worksheet with multiple data tables. Although you can create multiple PivotTables in a workbook, you can use only one table at a time when creating a PivotTable.

    - Remove any Excel generated subtotals or grand totals in the data by choosing Data⇨Subtotals⇨Remove All.

    - Plan your questions about how you want your data analyzed. For example, if your data is sales information, perhaps you want to know your sales totals by region or a specific salesperson, or even deeper such as by salesperson and by quarter. If your data is information about your video collection, perhaps your questions are how many DVDs you have with a certain actor as the star, or, how much you paid for all the PG-13 rated movies?

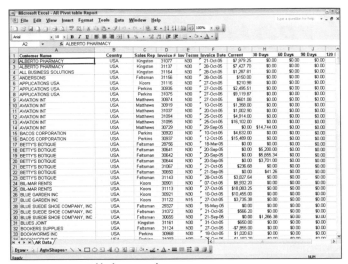

Figure 13-1: PivotTable data example

Figure 13-2: Separate multiple data ranges with blank rows and columns

2. Click in any cell containing data.

3. Choose Data➪PivotTable and PivotChart Report. Step 1 of the PivotTable and PivotChart Wizard appears. Excel needs to know where your data will come from:

- **Microsoft Excel List or Database:** Creates the PivotTable from organized data in a Microsoft Excel worksheet.

- **External Data Source:** Creates a PivotTable from data stored in a non-Excel database.

- **Multiple Consolidation Ranges:** Creates a PivotTable from multiple Microsoft Excel worksheet ranges.

- **Another PivotTable Report or PivotChart Report:** Creates a PivotTable from another PivotTable report in the same workbook.

4. Click the Next button. Step 2 appears.

5. Verify that Excel correctly identified your data range, including the headings. If not, specify the correct area in the Range box as you see in Figure 13-3.

6. Click the Next button. Step 3 appears.

7. Select the New Worksheet option.

 You can use the existing worksheet option if you're creating a PivotChart. You must create PivotTables as a new sheet in the existing workbook.

8. Click the Finish button. The PivotTable and PivotChart Wizard closes and Excel creates a new worksheet with a blank PivotTable, along with the PivotTable toolbar and the PivotTable Field List, which contains each field from your data range (see Figure 13-4). PivotTables contain four primary elements:

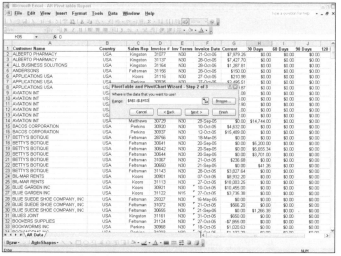

Figure 13-3: Specify the data you want to analyze

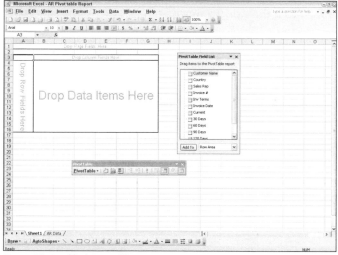

Figure 13-4: A blank PivotTable

- **Rows:** Displays your data vertically, with one item perrow.

- **Column:** Displays the data horizontally, with one item per column.

- **Data:** Summarizes the numerical data.

- **Page:** Displays each section of data on its own page, which allows you to display data for a single item.

9. From the PivotTable Field List, select the field you want categorized.

10. Select Row Area from the drop-down list at the bottom of the PivotTable Field List. Excel displays each unique item from the field you selected. In Figure 13-5, Excel displays each Sales Rep.

 If you want the categorized field displayed horizontally instead of vertically, choose Column Area instead of Row Area from the drop-down list.

11. Click the Add To button.

 Optionally, drag a field to its marked area, such as Add Rows Here. As you drag the field, your mouse pointer drags a small gray box.

12. From the PivotTable Field List, select the field you want summarized, such as sales totals.

13. Select Data Area from the drop-down list at the bottom of the PivotTable Field List. Excel takes the data and adds the totals to the PivotTable (see Figure 13-6).

 The PivotTable Field List indicates fields used in the PivotTable with bold lettering. You don't have to use all the fields in the PivotTable and you don't have to place fields in every area of the PivotTable.

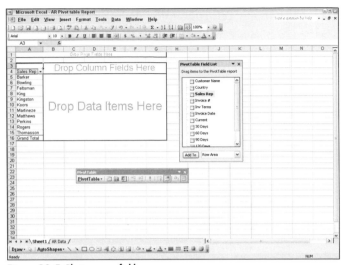

Figure 13-5: Placing a row field

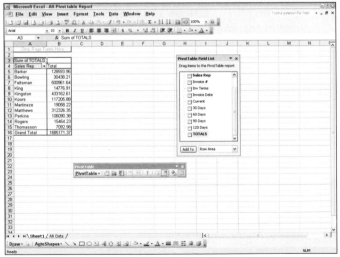

Figure 13-6: A completed PivotTable

Select and Manage Pivot Data

1. On the PivotTable, click the down arrow in the gray heading over the Row Fields section. A list of individual items appears.

 To remove any unwanted or misplaced field, select the gray heading and drag it off the PivotTable onto another area of the worksheet.

2. Remove the check mark next to any item you don't want included in the PivotTable.

 Optionally, to hide data in a PivotTable, right-click the field and choose Hide. Hiding an item removes it from the report, but the item still appears in the drop-down list for the field.

3. Click OK. In Figure 13-7, only data for two specifically selected sales reps appears in the PivotTable.

 Click the Show All option to quickly select or deselect all options.

4. Select any of the following methods to update the PivotTable with any changes made in the original data:

   • Click the Refresh Data button (as shown in Figure 13-8) or the PivotTable button on the PivotTable toolbar; then choose Refresh Data.

   • Right-click anywhere on the PivotTable and choose Refresh Data from the shortcut menu.

 To have the PivotTable refresh itself whenever you reopen the file, click the PivotTable button on the PivotTable toolbar and then choose Table Options. In the PivotTable Options dialog box, select Refresh on Open.

 Double-click any data value to display, on a new worksheet, the specific detail from which the data comprised.

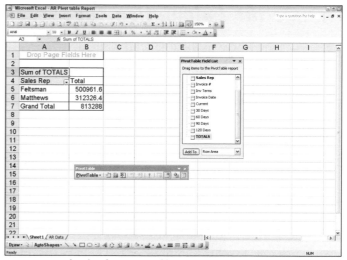

Figure 13-7: Filter data from a PivotTable

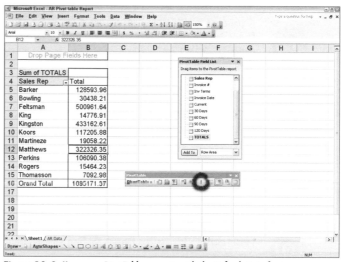

Figure 13-8: Keep your PivotTable accurate with the Refresh Data feature

Change the Calculation Type

1. Click anywhere in the totaled data field.

2. Click the Field Settings button on the PivotTable toolbar or right-click the field and choose Field Settings. The PivotTable Field dialog box, shown in Figure 13-9, appears.

3. From the Summarize By list, select the function you want to use. Choices include Sum, Count, Average, Max, Min, Product, CountNums, StdDev, StdDevp, Var, and Varp.

 Optionally, click the Number button and select a format for your summary field.

4. Click OK. Excel re-summarizes the field based on the function you selected. The field title also changes to reflect the selected function.

 If you don't want to display grand totals at the bottom, click the PivotTable button on the PivotTable toolbar and choose Table Options. From the PivotTable Options dialog box, remove the check mark from Grand Totals for Columns. Click OK.

AutoFormat PivotTables

1. From the PivotTable toolbar, click the Format Report button. The AutoFormat dialog box opens (see Figure 13-10).

2. Select a format and click OK.

 If you don't like any of the AutoFormat options, you can manually format any PivotTable section through the Field Settings feature.

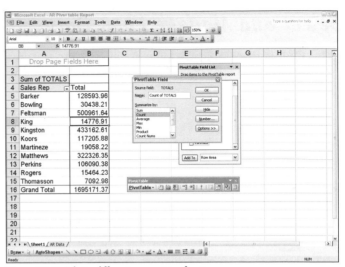

Figure 13-9: Select a different summarizing function

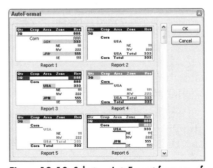

Figure 13-10: Select an AutoFormat from any of the many options

Apply Page Fields

1. From the PivotTable Field List, select the field you want to use to subdivide your PivotTable. For example, if you want to see the total sales of each sales rep by country, you select the Country field.

 Page fields allow you to filter the entire PivotTable report to display data for a single item or all the items.

2. Drag the field onto the Drop Page Fields Here section.

3. From the Page Field Selection drop-down list, select the field by which you want to filter. Figure 13-11 shows the sales total for the Canadian sales reps, instead of viewing all sales reps sales totals.

Generate Separate PivotTables

1. Save your file. The Undo function isn't available for this step, so if you don't get the results you expected, you have to manually delete each and every added worksheet.

2. From the Page Field Selection drop-down list, select the field by which you want to filter.

3. Click the PivotTable button on the PivotTable toolbar and choose Show Pages.

4. Click OK at the resulting Show Pages dialog box. As Figure 13-12 shows, Excel generates a PivotTable for each field (in this example, Country), each on its own worksheet in the workbook.

 To delete an unwanted separate PivotTable worksheet, right-click the unwanted worksheet tab and choose Delete. Click Delete again at the resulting confirmation message.

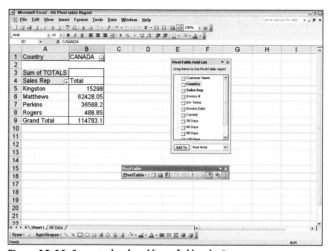

Figure 13-11: Separate data by adding a field to the Page area

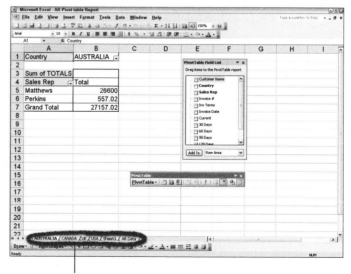

Worksheet tabs
Figure 13-12: Splitting the data into individual pages

Rename a Field

1. Select the field you want to rename.

2. Click the Field Settings button on the PivotTable toolbar. The PivotTable Field dialog box opens (see Figure 13-13).

 Optionally, click the field name in the PivotTable and begin typing a new name. Press Enter when you are finished.

3. Type the new name in the Name text box.

4. Click OK. Only the name on the PivotTable appears with the new name. The PivotTable Field List doesn't change.

Format PivotTable Values

1. Select the heading for the field you want to modify.

2. Click the Field Settings button on the PivotTable toolbar.

3. From the Field Settings dialog box, click the Number button.

4. From the Format Cells dialog box (see Figure 13-14), select the Number format you want.

5. If applicable, select the number of decimal places you want.

6. Click OK twice.

 To change the format of PivotTable text, select any desired text cells and format them with the tools on the Format toolbar or though the Excel Format Cells dialog box (choose Format➪Cells).

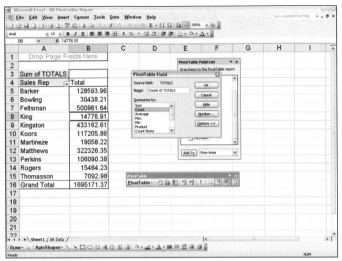

Figure 13-13: Rename a PivotTable field

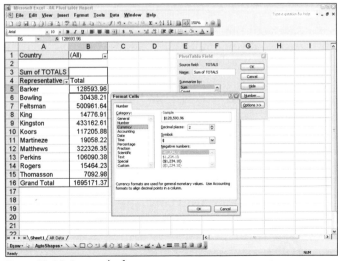

Figure 13-14: Setting value formats

Generate Multilevel Totals

1. Create a PivotTable (see the "Create a PivotTable" section, earlier in this chapter).

2. To create a second summary level, drag the next field you want to subtotal from the PivotTable Field List onto another PivotTable area, keeping these pointers in mind:

    *   If you want to create a second category, such as by Country, and then by Salesman, drag the field onto the Row area. Figure 13-15 shows a PivotTable with two categories. The field closest to the data is called the inner row (in this example, Sales Rep). The other field is called an outer row (in this example, Country). Excel displays data in the inner row under each of the outer row fields.

    *   If you want to total additional fields, drag the field into the Data area.

    *   If you want to sum different fields, or if you want to create two different total types (such as count and sum, or max and min), select a field you have already used. Currently used fields are listed in bold type. As you see in Figure 13-16, the fields appear vertically in the Data area.

     You can add even more data fields to your PivotTable. PivotTable data fields are only limited by the amount of memory in your computer.

    *   If you want the data fields displayed horizontally, drag the gray Data button onto the cell that has the Total heading. Excel rearranges the data fields.

     To redisplay the data in a vertical format, drag the Data button to the left, onto the Row area.

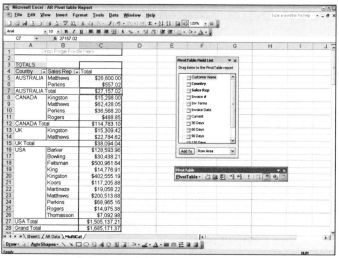

Figure 13-15: Multiple category fields

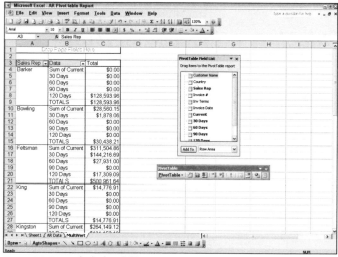

Figure 13-16: Multiple data fields

Group Data Together

1. Create a PivotTable (see the "Create a PivotTable" section, earlier in this chapter).

2. Click in any cell of the field you want to group. A popular field to group is a date field.

3. Click the PivotTable button on the PivotTable toolbar, and choose Group and Show Detail⇨Group.

4. From the Grouping dialog box, select the grouping option you want to use. The options that appear depend on the type of data you are grouping.

5. Click OK. Figure 13-17 illustrates two pivot table examples; one with the dates in detail and the other with the dates grouped together by month.

 To ungroup categories and redisplay the entire list, click the PivotTable button and choose Group and Show Detail⇨Ungroup.

Calculate a Percent of Totals

1. Add a second totals field and display the two fields horizontally (see the earlier section, "Generate Multilevel Totals").

2. Select the second totals field and click the Field Settings button on the PivotTable toolbar.

3. From the PivotTable Field dialog box (see Figure 13-18), choose % of Column from the Show Data As drop-down list.

4. Click OK. Excel displays the second totals field as a percent of total.

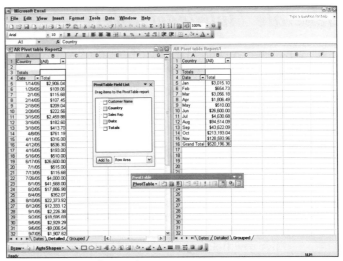

Figure 13-17: Group data together

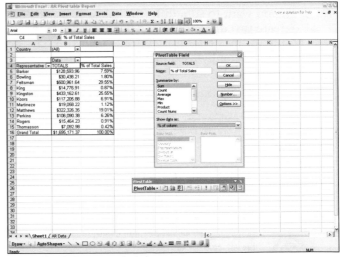

Figure 13-18: Create special calculations

Add Your Own Calculations

1. From the PivotTable toolbar, choose PivotTable⇨ Formulas⇨Calculated Field. The Insert Calculated Field dialog box appears.

2. In the Name text box, type a name for the formula, such as **CommAmt**.

 Calculated Field names can include spaces and special characters.

3. In the Formula box, delete the =0 and create your own formula, following these tips:

   - Like other Excel formulas, begin with an equal sign, but use field names instead of cell references.

    While you can't use cell references in a formula, you can use static values.

   - Double-click any field name in the Fields box to add it to the formula.

   - Use the standard formula operators such as plus, minus, multiply, and divide (+, –, *, and /). Figure 13-19 shows a formula that calculates a 12% commission on the sales rep totals.

4. Click OK. Excel creates a new data column with the calculated value. Figure 13-20 shows a PivotTable with a calculated field next to the data field.

 If you no longer want the calculated field on your PivotTable, drag the calculated field heading off the PivotTable, and onto another area of the worksheet.

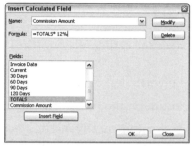

Figure 13-19: Create a customized calculation formula

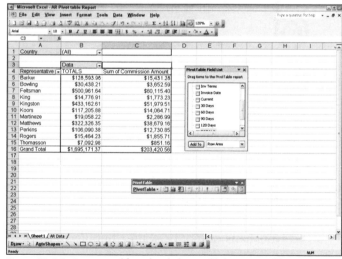

Figure 13-20: A customized formula calculation added to a PivotTable

Create a PivotChart

1. Create the PivotTable (see the earlier section, "Create a PivotTable").

2. Click anywhere in the PivotTable.

3. Click the PivotTable button on the PivotTable toolbar.

4. Choose PivotChart. Excel automatically inserts a new worksheet with a chart based on the PivotTable (see Figure 13-21). All PivotTable data, except for the totals and subtotals, appear in the PivotChart.

 Optionally, click the PivotChart button on the PivotTable toolbar.

 Changes to the PivotTable affect the PivotChart and field changes to the PivotChart affect the PivotTable.

5. Format the chart (see Chapter 9) with the following exceptions:

- You cannot move or resize the plot area.
- You cannot move or resize the legend.
- Refreshing the PivotTable removes any manually applied chart formatting.
- PivotCharts cannot be scatter, bubble, or stock charts.
- You cannot add data to the PivotChart from outside the PivotTable.
- You can use the PivotField buttons with the same functionality as those in the PivotTable. See Figure 13-22.

 To delete the PivotChart, right-click the chart sheet tab and choose Delete.

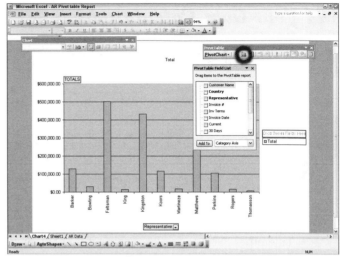

Figure 13-21: Create a PivotChart

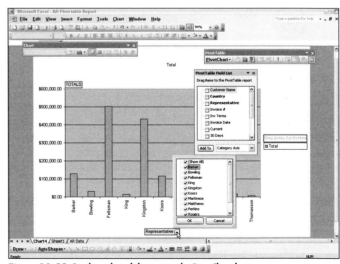

Figure 13-22: Display selected data using the PivotChart buttons

Building Simple Macros

*Y*ou can often save yourself time by automating tasks you perform frequently. The automation takes the form of an *Excel macro*, which is a series of commands and functions grouped together as a single command. Macros are created in a special programming language called Visual Basic and can be run whenever you need to perform the task.

While you can write your own very complex macros in the Visual Basic programming language, the easiest method for many macros is to use the Excel Macro Recorder. When you record a macro, Excel stores information about each step you take as you perform a series of commands. You then run the macro to repeat, or *play back*, the commands.

The macro recorder is very literal and records every action you complete. Therefore, planning your macro before you begin the recording process is very important so you don't record unnecessary steps.

Security is an important issue when working with macros, because if you open worksheets from other sources, the worksheets may contain macros that are harmful to your computer. By default, Excel protects you from running macros, but if you're creating your own macros, you'll probably need to change the security settings.

In this chapter, you find out how to change your security settings, as well as how to record, run, and delete Excel macros.

Chapter
14

Get ready to. . .

Record a Macro

1. Choose Tools⇨Macro⇨Record New Macro. The Record Macro dialog box, shown in Figure 14-1, appears.

2. In the Macro Name text box, type a name for the macro:

   - The first character of the macro name must be a letter.

   - Macro names cannot contain spaces. You can use letters, numbers, or the underscore character.

   - You cannot use a cell reference as a macro name.

   - Macro names are not case sensitive.

3. Select where you want to store the macro from the Store Macro In drop-down list:

   - **This Workbook:** Save the macro in the current workbook. If the file is a template, Excel stores the macro with the template. Any workbook using the template has access to the macro.

   - **New Workbook:** Create macros that run in any new workbooks created during the current Excel session.

   - **Personal Macro Workbook:** Choose this option if you want the macro to be available whenever you use Excel.

4. Type a description of the macro in the Description box. Click OK. A Stop Recording toolbar, as shown in Figure 14-2, appears on-screen.

5. Perform the actions you want to record.

 If you want to record the steps relative to the current cell, such as (Go up one row and insert a blank line), click the Relative Reference button on the Stop Recording toolbar.

6. Click the Stop Recording button or choose Tools⇨ Macro⇨Stop Recording.

Figure 14-1: The Record Macro dialog box

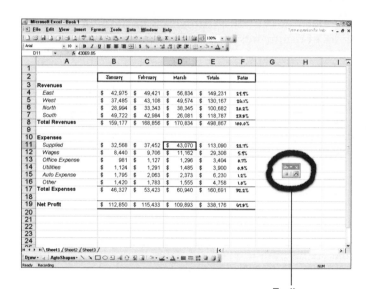

Figure 14-2: The Stop Recording toolbar

Toolbar

Check Macro Security Level

1. Choose Tools➪Macro➪Security. The Security dialog box shown in Figure 14-3 appears.

2. Set a security level:

   - **Very High:** Allows you to only run macros that are stored in a trusted location. The Trusted Publishers tab lists all trusted locations.

   - **High:** You can run only those macros that are digitally signed. This is the default setting in Excel.

    A digital signature is an electronic, encrypted, secure stamp of authentication obtained from a commercial certification authority. Excel's Visual Basic programming language contains a self-certifying digital signature tool, but because it doesn't come from a third party, Excel still considers it unauthenticated and displays a warning box.

   - **Medium:** Excel displays a dialog box asking if you want to enable macros. If you are creating your own macros, you should probably choose this setting.

   - **Low:** Allows macros to run without you being notified first. This can be helpful if you run a lot of macros, but be aware of the risk of using macros from unknown sources.

    Select the Low setting only if you have virus scanning software that checks your Microsoft Office files or you open only workbooks that you know do not contain viruses.

3. Click OK.

4. Close any currently open Excel workbooks. Depending on the setting you selected, when you reopen a file containing a macro, you may see the Security Warning dialog box, shown in Figure 14-4.

5. Click the Enable Macros button if you know where the macro originated.

Figure 14-3: The Security dialog box

Figure 14-4: Macro warning box

Run a Macro

1. Choose Tools➪Macro➪Macros. The Macro dialog box, shown in Figure 14-5, appears.

2. Select the macro you want to run.

3. Click the Run button. Excel executes the selected macro.

 Save your file before running a newly created macro. You cannot undo the macro.

Figure 14-5: Select a prerecorded macro

Assign a Macro KeyStroke

1. Click Tools➪Macro➪Record New Macro.

2. In the Macro Name text box, type a name for the macro.

3. Select where you want to store the macro from the Store Macro In drop-down list.

4. Type a description of the macro in the Description box.

5. Assign a keystroke combination (see Figure 14-6). If you select a shortcut key already used in Excel, the macro shortcut overrides the Excel shortcut while the workbook that contains the macro is open.

Figure 14-6: Assign a shortcut key to a macro

 If you enter a lowercase letter, Excel assigns it a Ctrl+lowercase letter combination. If you type an uppercase letter, you must press Ctrl+Shift+the letter to run the macro. The shortcut key cannot be a number or special character.

6. Click OK.

7. Perform the actions you want to record and then click the Stop Recording button.

8. To execute the macro, press the shortcut key you assigned.

Create a Macro Toolbar Button

1. Choose Tools⇨Customize.

2. Click the Commands tab. Then select Macros from the Categories list.

3. Drag the Custom button from the Commands box to the toolbar on which you want to place it.

4. Release the mouse button when the mouse pointer resembles a capital letter I like the one in Figure 14-7.

5. With the new button selected, click the Modify Selection button in the Customize dialog box.

6. Choose Assign Macro. The Assign Macro dialog box appears.

7. Select the macro you want to assign to the toolbar button.

8. Click OK.

9. Click the Close button.

10. To run the macro, simply click the toolbar button.

 Check out Chapter 15 for more information on customizing toolbars.

Stop a Macro

1. Press the Escape key. The Microsoft Visual Basic window opens (see Figure 14-8).

2. Click the End button.

 Hold the Shift key while starting Excel to prevent Excel from automatically running a macro.

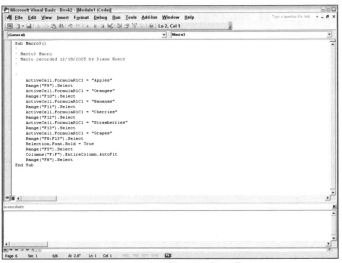

Figure 14-7: Quickly access a macro by adding it to the toolbar

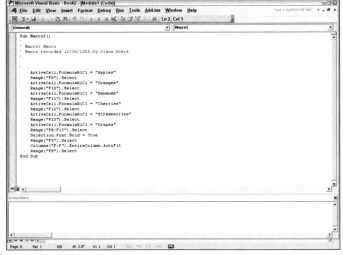

Figure 14-8: Stopping a macro

Delete a Macro

1. Open the workbook containing the macro you want to delete.

2. Choose Tools⇨Macro⇨Macros. The Macro dialog box appears (see Figure 14-9).

3. From the Macro dialog box, select the macro name you want to delete.

4. Click the Delete button. A confirmation box appears.

5. Click Yes.

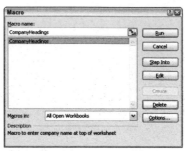

Figure 14-9: Select a macro to delete

 Deleting a macro does not remove any button you placed on the toolbar. To delete a button from the toolbar, choose Tools⇨Customize and drag the button off the toolbar.

Delete a Personal Macro

1. Choose Window⇨Unhide. The Unhide dialog box, shown in Figure 14-10, appears (unless the Personal Workbook already is displayed or you don't have any personal Macros).

2. Choose Personal, then click OK. The Personal Workbook appears.

3. Choose Tools⇨Macro⇨Macros. From the Macro dialog box, select the macro you want to delete.

4. Click the Delete button. A confirmation box appears.

5. Click Yes.

6. Choose File⇨Close. (You are closing the Personal Workbook.) A Save Confirmation dialog box appears.

7. Click Yes.

Figure 14-10: Unhide the Personal Workbook

Saving Time with Excel Tools

*T*his chapter is about stuff . . . Excel stuff. In the earlier chapters, I show how Excel has lots of power to make your computing life a little easier. This chapter contains a diverse group of Excel tools designed to speed up data entry and help improve spreadsheet quality.

In this chapter you discover how to

➠ Add special characters such as the copyright symbol, the registered trademark, foreign characters, or smiley faces.

➠ Create a custom toolbar where you can specify the tools you use most often.

➠ Split data into multiple columns where you can break up data containing multiple words such as a first name and last name; or city, state, and zip code into separate columns.

➠ Merge columns, which uses the Excel CONCATENATE function to combine data.

➠ Manage Excel's *AutoCorrect feature*, where you see how Excel automatically corrects many common misspelling or formatting issues.

➠ Work with *SmartTags*, those funny little indicators that often appear when you perform certain Excel functions or enter a particular type of Excel data.

➠ Let Excel flag potential formula errors and offer to correct them for you.

Chapter 15

Get ready to. . .

Add Special Characters

1. Click where you want the symbol. Special characters can be in their own cell or amid other text or values.

2. Choose Insert⇨Symbol. The Symbol dialog box appears (see Figure 15-1).

3. From the Symbols tab, click the symbol you want to use.

 Different fonts display different symbols. If you don't see the symbol you want, select a different font from the Font drop-down list. Additional special characters are available on the Special Characters tab.

4. Click the Insert button. Excel inserts the symbol into the current cell. Click the Close button.

Create a Custom Toolbar

1. Choose Tools⇨Customize. The Customize dialog box appears.

2. From the Toolbars tab, click the New button.

3. Enter the name you want to describe the new toolbar.

4. Click OK. A new blank toolbar appears on-screen.

5. From the Commands tab of the Customize dialog box, select a category for the first tool you want to add. A list of available Excel commands appears on the right side of the dialog box (see Figure 15-2).

6. Drag the command you want until it is on top of the new toolbar. When you release the mouse button, a button representing the command appears on the new toolbar.

7. Click the Close button.

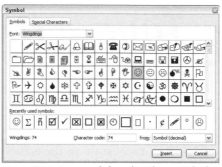

Figure 15-1: Insert symbols, such as the copyright character, into a cell

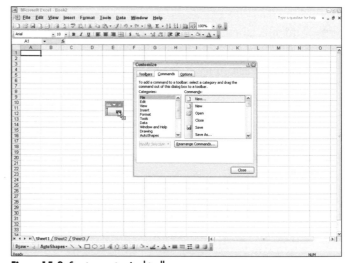

Figure 15-2: Create a customized toolbar

Split Data into Multiple Columns

1. Insert blank columns to the left of the cells you want to convert into multiple columns. If you want your data in three columns, then you must have two blank columns.

2. Select the cells you want to convert.

> You can't split empty cells, and you can't split merged cells. You must first unmerge the cells. See Chapter 4 for information about merged cells.

3. Choose Data➪Text to Columns. The Convert Text to Columns Wizard appears (see Figure 15-3).

4. Select the Original data type that suits your date. The Delimited type works if your data has a similar format. If the cells all contain a specific number of characters, select the Fixed Width radio button.

> If your data type is delimited, be sure that each section is separated by a common character such as a comma, period, apostrophe, or tab.

5. Click Next. The option you see next depends on which data type you selected in Step 4. For Fixed Width, click the ruler bar where you want the data to split. For Delimited, enter the character you used to separate your text. In Figure 15-4, the text is separated by a space.

6. Click the Finish button. Excel separates the selected cells into multiple columns.

7. Click OK.

> To split data into two lines in the same cell, press Alt+Enter where you want to break the line.

Figure 15-3: Convert text to multiple columns by specifying what separates the text sections

Figure 15-4: Splitting data into multiple columns

Merge Columns

1. Click in the cell where you want the merged data.

2. Choose Insert⇨Function.

3. From the Category drop-down list, choose Text.

4. Select CONCATENATE. (See Figure 15-5.)

5. Click OK. The Function Arguments dialog box appears.

6. Type the first cell address or click the cell you want to add to the combination. Excel enters the cell address in the Text1 box.

 Optionally, on any line, if you want specific text that's not in a cell address, type the text or punctuation, including any spaces. Excel places any spaces, punctuation, or text in quotation marks.

7. In the Text2 box, click the cell or type the text you want next. Each element must go in its own Text box line. Figure 15-6 shows an example.

8. Click OK.

 To convert the merged cells into plain text, instead of formulas, select the merged cells, choose Edit⇨Copy, choose Edit⇨Paste Special, and then select Values from the Paste Special dialog box.

 Optionally, use the ampersand (&) between cell addresses to join text items. For example, =A1&B1 returns the same value as =CONCATENATE(A1,B1). However, the cells you connect with the ampersand cannot be blank.

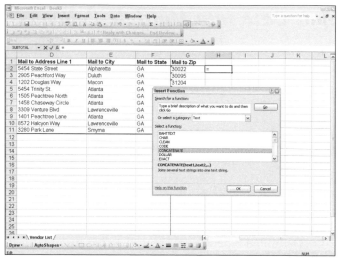

Figure 15-5: Using a function to combine multiple columns into a single column

Figure 15-6: Concatenating text columns

Manage AutoCorrect

1. Choose Tools⇨AutoCorrect Options. The AutoCorrect Options dialog box opens.

2. Remove the check marks from any option you do not want Excel to automatically correct.

3. In the Replace box, type a common typing mistake. For example, if you frequently type *profitt* instead of *profit,* type **profitt** in the Replace box.

4. In the With text box, type the correct word (see Figure 15-7).

5. Click the Add button.

To remove any unwanted entry, select the entry and click the Delete button.

6. Click the AutoFormat As You Type tab.

7. Remove the check mark from any feature you don't want Excel to automatically perform.

8. Click OK.

Figure 15-7: AutoCorrect Options

Check for Formula Errors

1. Choose Tools⇨Error Checking. Excel checks the current worksheet for formula errors and stops at the first error. As Figure 15-8 shows, the Error Checking dialog box offers several pieces of information including the cell reference containing the possible problem, a description of the possible problem, and a button to remedy the problem.

2. Click the button that offers to remedy the problem or Next to leave the formula as is.

3. When the error checking is complete, click OK.

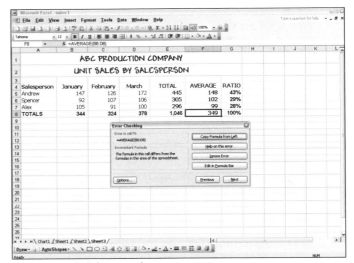

Figuro 15-8: Check for potential errors

Work with SmartTags

1. Choose Tools⇨AutoCorrect Options.

2. Click the SmartTags tab (see Figure 15-9).

3. Enable the Label Data with SmartTags option.

4. Click OK.

 To have Excel notify you with a sound whenever a SmartTag appears, you must have Microsoft Office Sounds installed on your computer. Then choose Tools⇨Options and from the General tab, select the Provide Feedback with Sound option.

5. From the worksheet, click a SmartTag icon. Each SmartTag type appears with a different icon appearance including

   - **Paste:** These appear over pasted data (such as the one in Figure 15-10), offering options about pasting.

   - **AutoFill:** These appear after you fill data in a worksheet, offering how to fill the text or data.

   - **Insert:** These appear next to inserted cells, rows, or columns, offering a list of formatting options.

   - **AutoCorrect:** These appear as a small, blue box near text that was automatically corrected, offering to undo an AutoCorrect action.

   - **Financial:** These appear over a cell with a U.S. stock symbol and offers options to check stock prices. Financial SmartTags are indicated by a purple triangle in the lower-right corner of a worksheet cell.

   - **Error Checking:** These appear over potential formula errors in the same way as the Error Checking feature. Error Checking SmartTags are indicated by a small green triangle in the upper-left corner of a worksheet cell.

Figure 15-9: Enable additional SmartTags

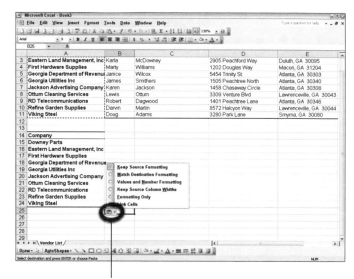

Smart Tag icon

Figure 15-10: Paste SmartTag options

Part V
Practical Applications for Excel

The 5th Wave   By Rich Tennant

"That's it! We're getting a wireless network for the house."

Creating a Commission Calculator

Suppose you're a business owner and you pay your salespeople a sliding commission rate based on their total sales for a specified period, such as a month. First, you need a sheet of paper to list each salesperson's sales. Then, at the end of the period, you have to subtotal each person's sales. Finally, you have to figure out which percent commission to give based on that subtotal.

With a Commission Calculator worksheet, designed with the use of basic Excel features, as well as using several Excel functions (SUMIF, COUNTIF, and nested IF statements), all you have to do is enter the individual sales. Excel does the rest for you, saving you precious time and reducing the chance for human error. To set a worksheet up, you do the following tasks:

➡ Enter basic headings

➡ Create a sliding commission rate table

➡ Define the data input area where you track the individual sales

➡ Design the calculation area where Excel calculates the totals and commission

➡ Enhance the worksheet appearance so it's easier to read

➡ Protect and save the worksheet as a template

Enter Headings

1. In cell A1, type **Commission Calculator**.

2. In cell A2, type **For the month of:**.

3. In cells A3, B3, C3, and D3, type the following column headings: **Sales Person**, **# of Sales**, **Total Sales Amount**, and **Commission Amount**.

4. Move down enough rows to accommodate all your salespeople's names, plus a couple of extra rows, and in column A of the row, type **Totals**.

5. Beginning with cell A4, moving down the column, list the names of your salespeople.

6. Move down three more rows and type the following column headings: **Sale Date**, **Transaction Number**, **Sales Person**, **Sale Amount**. Your worksheet should look like Figure 16-1.

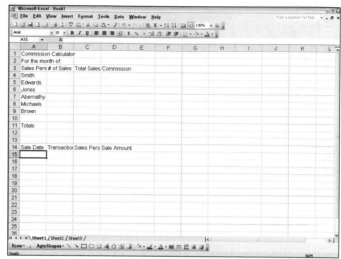

Figure 16-1: Enter headings for a commission worksheet

Create the Commission Table

1. In an unused area of the worksheet, enter your sales dollar breakdown.

2. In the cells next to the sales dollar breakdown, such as in cells L4, L5, L6, and so forth, enter the commission percentage.

3. Format the sales dollar values as currency (see Chapter 4).

4. Format the commissions as percentages (see Figure 16-2).

5. Select the commission table and choose Insert⇨Name⇨ Define. The Define Name dialog box appears.

6. Type **CommissionTable** or another name for the table.

7. Click OK.

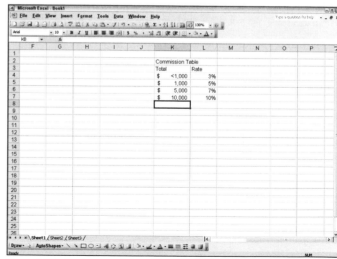

Figure 16-2: Create a commission table

Define the Sales Data Input Area

1. At the bottom of the worksheet where you will enter the individual sales, select the cells in the Salesperson column. In Figure 16-3, I selected cells C15 through C114, which gives room for 100 sales entries.

2. Choose Insert⇨Name⇨Define. The Define Name dialog box appears.

3. Type **SalesRep** for the range name; then click OK.

4. In the same worksheet section, select the cells you will use in the Sales Amount column. Be sure to include the same number of cells you included in Step 1.

5. Choose Insert⇨Name⇨Define. The Define Name dialog box appears.

6. Type **SalesAmt** for the range name; then click OK.

 To verify the formulas you create in the next several sections, enter some sample data in the sales data input area.

Total Sales with the SUMIF Function

1. In cell C4, enter the following formula and then press Enter: **=SUMIF(SalesRep,A4,SalesAmt)**. If you entered sample data in the sales data input area, you see the total sales for the salesperson.

 The Excel SUMIF function calculates the totals of numbers that meet specified criteria. The function first asks for the area you want to look at, then the cell it should look to match, and finally the amount you want the function to total.

2. Copy the formula in C4 to the end of your salesperson list (see Figure 16-4). Chapter 2 shows how to copy formulas.

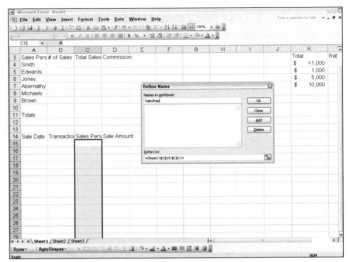

Figure 16-3: Define the sales person data input area

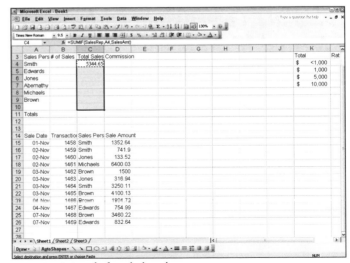

Figure 16-4: Copy the formula down the rows

Use the COUNTIF Function to Count Sales

1. In cell B4, enter the following formula, then press Enter: **=COUNTIF(SalesRep,A4)**. If you entered sample data in the sales data input area, you see the total number of sales for the salesperson.

 The Excel COUNTIF function counts the number of entries that meet specified criteria. The function first asks for the area you want to look at, then the cell it should look to match.

2. Select cell B4 and choose Edit⇨Copy.

3. Highlight cells B5 through the end of your salesperson list.

4. Choose Edit⇨Paste. Excel duplicates the formulas to include all the salespeople. (See Figure 16-5.)

Calculate Commission with a Nested IF Statement

1. In cell D4, enter the beginning function and the first parameter to check the total sales for the sales person against the commission table. Type **=IF(C4<K5** and a comma.

 If you created your commission table in a different location, change the cell references to match your commission table.

 Be sure to place the dollar signs in front of the cell references to make them an absolute reference to a specific cell.

2. Enter the first True result. Type **C4*L4** and a comma.

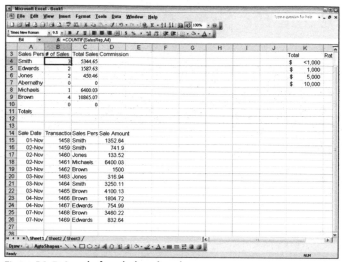

Figure 16-5: Copy the formula throughout the rows

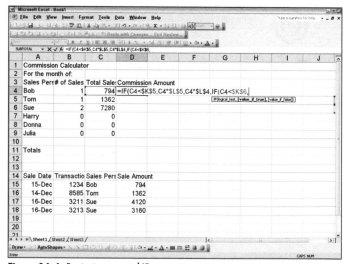

Figure 16-6: Beginning a nested IF statement

3. Enter the first False result that begins another IF statement. Type **IF(C4<K6** and a comma (see Figure 16-6).

4. Enter the next True result. Type **C4*L5** and a comma.

5. Enter the next False result that again begins another IF statement. Type **IF(C4<K7** and a comma.

6. Enter the third True result, if applicable. Type **C4*L6** and a comma.

7. Enter the third False result, which in my example is the last level to check. Type **C4*L7**.

8. Type three closing parentheses, enough to match the number of opening parentheses and press Enter. Figure 16-7 illustrates the final formula and its results.

9. Copy the formula to the other rows.

The Excel IF function evaluates a condition you specify, and returns one value if the statement is TRUE and another value if it evaluates to FALSE. In this example, if the sales are less than the first commission level, making the first condition TRUE, it calculates the sales multiplied by the first level commission percentage. If the statement is not TRUE, then Excel checks if the sales are less than a second commission level, and if so, it multiplies the sales times that commission level percentage. The nesting continues until Excel checks all commission levels, resulting in a commission amount.

Create Totals

1. In cell B11, or the cell below your last sales rep, create a SUM function to total the cells above it. In Figure 16-8, the formula =SUM(B4:B10) totals the sales orders.

2. Select the formula in cell B11 and choose Edit⇨Copy.

3. Select the cells C11 and D11 and choose Edit⇨Paste. Excel duplicates the formulas, which total the sales and commissions, respectively.

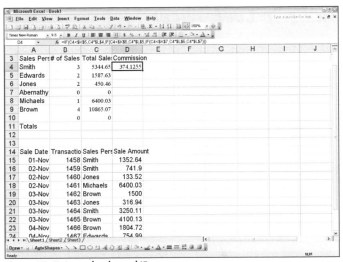

Figure 16-7: A completed nested IF statement

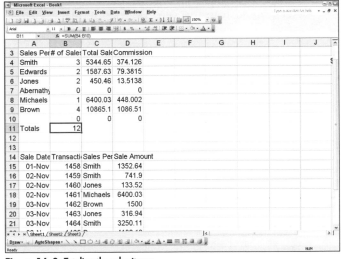

Figure 16-8: Totaling the sales items

Make It Look Nicer

1. Apply currency number formatting to cells with currency.

2. Widen columns to allow all cell data to appear.

3. Bold the headings.

4. Make the headings a larger font.

5. Apply borders as desired.

6. Merge and center cells A2 and B2.

7. Click the Right Align button to right align the data.

8. Merge and center cells C2 and D2.

9. Click the Left Align button to left align the data.

10. Add a light color shading to every other row as shown in Figure 16-9.

11. Choose Tools⇨Options. From the View tab, remove the check mark from the Zero Values option.

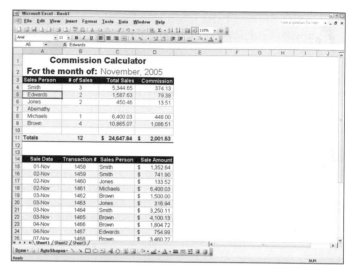

Figure 16-9: Alternate row shading makes a spreadsheet easier to read

Protect Your Work

1. Select the cells in which you will enter the entry month and the sales data.

2. Choose Format⇨Cells.

3. On the Protection tab, deselect the Locked option (as shown in Figure 16-10) and click OK.

4. Choose Tools⇨Protection⇨Protect Sheet.

5. Click OK.

 Save the worksheet as a template to protect it from changes. (See Chapter 7.)

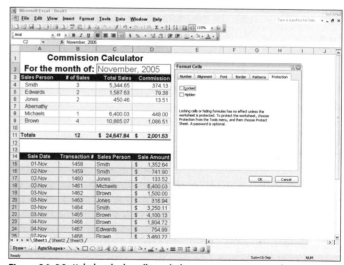

Figure 16-10: Unlock only the cells in which you want users to enter data

Tracking Medical Expenses

Chapter 17

With today's high cost of medical care, very few of us can be without medical insurance. In fact, many of us have two insurance companies, perhaps Medicare and a supplemental insurance, or insurance through your employer and your spouse's employer.

Tracking medical costs is very important, especially when filing your annual tax return. In this project, you create an Excel spreadsheet that efficiently tracks your expenses, generating totals, even sorting out prescriptions from the rest of the medical expense totals. See at a glance how much your medical expenses total, how much is paid by your insurance companies, and — most important of all — how much you have to pay out of your pocket.

To accomplish this task, you use a number of Excel features including data validation, duplication of worksheets, creating totals from other worksheets, and a few Excel mathematical functions, too.

Hopefully your health is well and you won't need to use this worksheet a lot! But if you do . . . you'll be glad it's here.

Get ready to . . .

Enter Text Headings

1. In cell A1, enter a heading for the worksheet.

2. In cells B4 and B5, type **Total Billed** and **Total Paid by Insurance**, respectively.

3. In cells D4 and D5, type **Total Paid Out of Pocket** and **Total Due**, respectively.

4. In cell D7, type **Totals**.

5. In cells A8 through K8, type the following: **Bill Date, Provider, Rx?, Description of Services, Total Amount Billed, Insurance #1 Paid, Insurance #2 Paid, Write Off, Paid Out of Pocket, Check Number**, and **Amount Due**. Your worksheet should look similar to Figure 17-1.

Create Totaling Formulas

1. In cell E7, enter a formula to calculate the entire Total Amount Billed column **=SUM(E9:E50)**. Make the formula longer or shorter depending on such as the items you have.

2. Select cell E7 again, and grab the AutoFill handle and drag across to cell K7. This duplicates the formula from F7 through K7. (See Figure 17-2.)

3. Select cell J7 and press Delete to delete the formula.

4. In cell C4, which references the total amount billed shown in cell E7, type **=E7**.

5. In cell C5, type **=F7+G7**, which adds the insurance payments together.

6. In cell E4, type **=I7** to reference the total out of pocket expenses.

7. In cell E5, type **=K7** to reference the total still due.

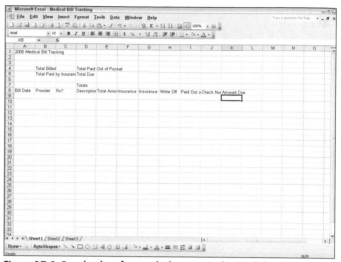

Figure 17-1: Enter headings for a medical expense tracking worksheet

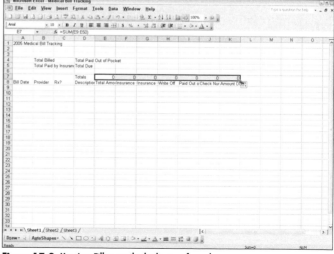

Figure 17-2: Use AutoFill to easily duplicate a formula

Calculate the Amount Due

1. Create a formula in cell K9 that subtracts the total of the payments made from the total amount billed by typing =E9-SUM(F9:I9).

> Notice in Step 1, the compound formula created with a standard reference and an Excel function.

2. Select cell K9.

3. Choose Edit⇨Copy a marquee appears.

4. Click and drag from cell K10 through the end of your calculation area. Use the same amount of rows as in Step 1 of the section "Create Totaling Formulas".

5. Choose Edit⇨Paste. Excel copies the formula. Figure 17-3 shows a value of 0 in each pasted cell.

Specify Data Validation

1. In two adjacent cells, preferably in an unseen area, type **Yes** and **No**.

2. Select cells C9 through C50, or whichever row you use as your last worksheet row.

3. Choose Data⇨Validation.

4. From the Allow drop-down list, choose List.

5. Click the spreadsheet icon in the Source box. The Data Validation dialog box temporarily collapses.

6. Highlight cells Q1 and Q2, or whichever cells you used in Steps 1 and 2, and press Enter. The Data Validation dialog box reappears, as shown in Figure 17-4.

7. Click OK. Notice when you click cell C9 or lower, a drop-down arrow appears with the Yes or No choices.

Figure 17-3: Copy the Amount Due formula

Figure 17-4: Setting a Yes or No validation answer for the Rx column

Format the Worksheet

1. Highlight worksheet cells you want to format.

2. Apply any desired formatting such as applying currency or number formatting, widening columns, bolding headings, and applying borders. See Chapter 4. Figure 17-5 illustrates a formatting example.

Determine Print Settings

1. Choose File⇨Page Setup. Excel displays the Page Setup dialog box.

2. On the Page tab, select Landscape, choose the Fit To option, and make it 1 page wide by 1 page tall.

 Depending on the number of rows in your sheet, you may want to make the settings more than 1 page tall.

3. Click the Margins tab and enter .5 for each margin.

4. Click the Center on Page Horizontally option.

5. Click the Header/Footer tab and click the Custom Footer button.

6. In the Left section, type **Page &[Page] of &[Pages]**. Optionally, click the Page Number and Number of Pages buttons.

7. Click OK.

8. On the Sheet tab (shown in Figure 17-6), click in the Print Area text box and type **A1:K50** (or however many rows you anticipate using).

9. Click OK to close the Page Setup dialog box.

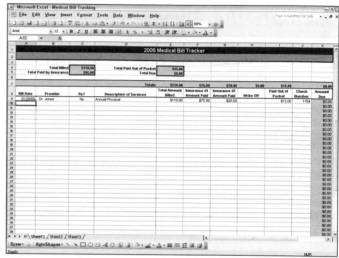

Figure 17-5: Apply formatting to your worksheet to make it easier to read

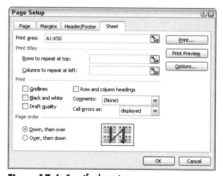

Figure 17-6: Specify the print area

Add Protection from Accidental Changes

1. Select cells A1 and A2. Choose Format⇨Cells.

2. From the Protection tab, remove the check mark from the Locked option. Click OK.

3. Select cells A9 through J50 (the data entry area). Choose Format⇨Cells.

4. From the Protection tab, remove the check mark from the Locked option. Click OK.

5. Choose Tools⇨Protection⇨Protect Sheet. The Protect Sheet dialog box, shown in Figure 17-7, opens.

6. Click OK.

Figure 17-7: Protect your worksheet from accidental changes

Duplicate the Worksheet for Other Family Members

1. In cell A2, type the patient's name.

2. Right-click the Sheet1 tab and choose Rename. The Sheet1 name is highlighted.

3. Type the patient's name. Press Enter. Excel renames the worksheet.

4. Right-click the newly renamed tab and choose Move or Copy.

5. Click the Create a Copy option. (See Figure 17-8.)

6. Click OK. Excel adds a copy of the sheet.

7. Right-click the new worksheet tab and rename it to the second patient's name.

8. In the second patient worksheet, click cell A2 and enter the second patient's name.

Figure 17-8: Duplicate the worksheet for each family member

Create a Totals Worksheet

1. Rename the tab of Sheet2 (or any blank worksheet in the workbook) to Totals.

2. From one of the patient worksheets, copy cells A1 and A2 to cells A1 and A2 on the Totals worksheet.

3. From one of the patient worksheets, copy cells E8 through I8 to cells E8 through I8 on the Totals worksheet.

4. Widen the columns as needed to see the text.

5. In cell A2, type the word **Totals**.

6. In cell C8, type the words **Patient Name**.

7. In cell D8, type the word **Service**. (See Figure 17-9.)

8. In cells C9 and C10, type the first patient's name.

9. In cell D9, type **Rx**.

10. In cell D10, type **Other**.

11. In cell D11, type **Totals**. (See Figure 17-10.)

12. In cells E9 through I11, type the formulas in the following table, substituting Mary for the first patient worksheet tab name.

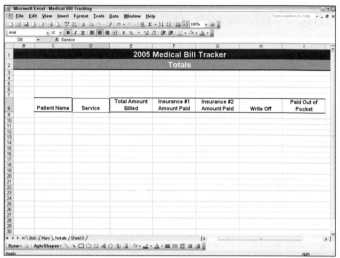

Figure 17-9: Entering headings on the Totals worksheet

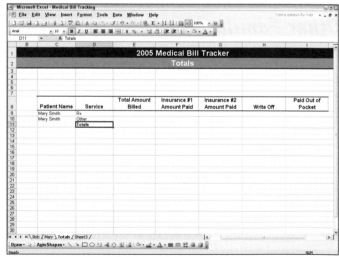

Figure 17-10: Preparing the Totals worksheet

In Cell	Type
E9	=SUMIF(Mary!C:C,"Yes",Mary!E:E)
E10	=SUMIF(Mary!C:C,"No",Mary!E:E
E11	=SUM(E9:E10)
F9	=SUMIF(Mary!C:C,"Yes",Mary!F:F)

In Cell	Type
F10	=SUMIF(Mary!C:C,"No",Mary!F:F
F11	=SUM(F9:F10)
G9	=SUMIF(Mary!C:C,"Yes",Mary!G:G)
G10	=SUMIF(Mary!C:C,"No",Mary!G:G
G11	=SUM(G9:G10)
H9	=SUMIF(Mary!C:C,"Yes",Mary!H:H)
H10	=SUMIF(Mary!C:C,"No",Mary!H:H
H11	=SUM(H9:H10)
I9	=SUMIF(Mary!C:C,"Yes",Mary!I:I)
I10	=SUMIF(Mary!C:C,"No",Mary!I:I
I11	=SUM(I9:I10)

13. Repeat Steps 8 through 12 for each patient. Figure 17-11 illustrates data entered into the Mary worksheet and how the totals reflect in the Totals worksheet.

14. Click cell A1and choose Format➪Cells.

15. From the Protection tab, remove the check mark from Locked.

16. Click OK.

17. Choose Tools➪Protection➪Protect Sheet.

18. Click OK. The worksheet is now protected against accidental changes.

Figure 17-11: The Medical Bill Tracker worksheet with sample data

 These formulas look at column C on the patient worksheet, and determine if the expense is a prescription. It then adds the values together.

 If you need to unprotect the sheet to make changes, choose Tools➪ Protection➪Unprotect Sheet.

 Save and use the workbook as a template! See the next section to do so.

Save the Workbook as a Template

1. Delete any data in the patient worksheets.

2. Choose File⇨Save As. The Save As dialog box appears, as shown in Figure 17-12.

3. From the Save as Type drop-down list, choose Template.

4. Click the Save button.

5. Close the template. You can now safely enter data into a blank Medical Bill Tracker without danger of modifying the original template and its formulas.

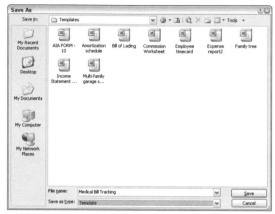

Figure 17-12: Save the workbook as a template

Planning for Your Financial Future

*Y*our life is taking shape right in front of you. You and your spouse want to buy a house, raise a family, and spend life happily ever after. Your personal future depends a lot on your financial future. Fortunately, Excel has several functions you can use to plan for the future you want.

First, to keep up your expectations, you need to determine how much house you can afford to buy. But before you can buy the dream house, you know you need to pay off some credit card debt. Next, from you own experience, you know that college is expensive, and the costs are bound to get much higher by the time the kids are ready. Finally will come your golden years. You dream of the house on the beach or traveling to exotic places.

How are you ever going to save enough for that? This chapter shows you how to

➡ Determine how much payments will run on that cute little ranch house down the street. Excel has a PMT function to help with that.

➡ Plan to pay off a credit card balance using the NPER function, which requires three key pieces of information: the interest rate, the current payment amount, and the credit card balance.

➡ Determine how much you need to save each month to reach a college fund or retirement goal. Again, utilize Excel's PMT function.

Plan for a House

1. In cell A1, type **OUR DREAM HOUSE.**

2. In cells A3 through A8, type **House Price, Down Payment, Loan Amount, Interest Rate, Loan Term,** and **Monthly Payment.**

3. In cell B3, enter the house price.

4. In cell B4, enter the down payment amount.

5. In cell B5, enter the formula **=B3-B4.** This gives the amount you will finance.

6. In cell B6, enter the interest rate. Format this amount as a percentage.

7. In cell B7, enter the loan term. Usually for a house, this value is in years. See Figure 18-1.

8. In cell B8, enter a PMT function to calculate the monthly payment. The PMT function has three required arguments (=PMT(RATE, NETPER, PV) so you need to enter **=PMT(B6/12,B7*12,B5).** See Figure 18-2.

   - RATE is the annual interest rate. You entered the interest rate in cell B6. To get a monthly rate, you divide this argument by 12.

   - NETPER is the term of the loan that you entered in cell B7. Because this value is in years, and you want monthly payments, you multiply this argument by 12.

   - PV represents the present value that is the amount you will finance, not including interest. You calculated this amount in cell B5.

 When you type the start of a function, Excel displays a yellow box containing a list of the arguments used by the function. Arguments in brackets are optional.

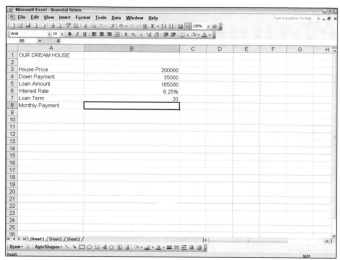

Figure 18-1: Enter the values needed to calculate a home loan payment

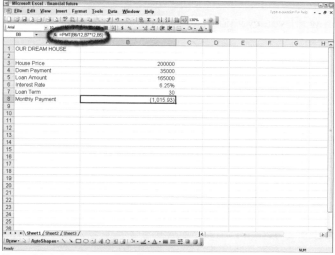

Figure 18-2: Using the Excel PMT function

Prepare to Pay Off a Credit Card Balance

1. In cell D1, type **PAY OFF CREDIT CARD.**

2. In cells D3, D4, and D5, type **Monthly percentage rate, Current payments, Credit card balance,** and **Months until paid off,** respectively.

3. In cell E3, create a formula to enter the *monthly* percentage rate you are paying on a credit card. For example if you are paying a 21% annual interest, you enter **=21%/12.** Excel displays a value of .0175, which is the 21% annual rate divided by 12 months. (See Figure 18-3.)

4. In cell E4, enter your current payment amount, preceded with a minus sign. Enter **-125** if you are making $125 payments every month against the credit card balance.

5. In cell E5, enter the remaining balance on the credit card. Like the payments, this must be entered as a negative value such as **-3700.**

6. Create an NPER formula to calculate how many months you need to pay off the credit card. The formula should read **=NPER(E3,E4,E5)**. As you see in Figure 18-4, the resulting answer shows how many months it will take to pay off the credit card balance. The NPER function has three required arguments:

   • Interest rate is usually given annually, so you divide it by 12 to give a monthly rate.

   • Payment amount that you enter as a negative amount.

   • Present value is the amount of the loan, not including interest.

7. Apply any desired formatting to the cells.

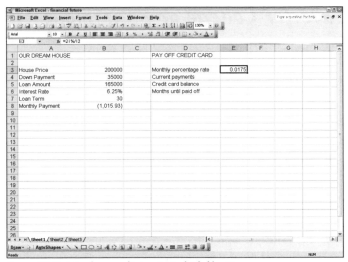

Figure 18-3: Enter the annual interest rate divided by 12

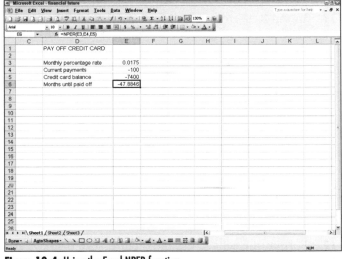

Figure 18-4: Using the Excel NPER function

Save for College or Retirement

1. In cell A12, type **OUR SAVINGS GOALS**.

2. In cell A14, type **Savings Goal Amount**.

3. In cell A15, type **Interest Rate**.

4. In cell A16, type **Years to Goal**.

5. In cell A17, type **Current Savings**.

6. In cell A18, type **Monthly Amount to Save**. See Figure 18-5.

7. In cell B14, enter the savings goal amount.

8. In cell B15, enter the annual interest rate.

9. In cell B16, enter the number of years you have until you will need the money for college or retirement.

10. In cell B17, enter the amount you already have saved toward the goal.

11. In cell B18, create a PMT formula that includes the interest rate, term, and amount. You also need to add one of the optional arguments: the future value argument. This time, the PMT formula format is =PMT(interest rate, term, current value, future value) so you should enter **=PMT(=PMT(B15/12, B16*12,B17,B14)**. The PMT function actually has two optional arguments:

    • Future Value is the balance of the loan after all payments have been made. You do not need to enter a future value unless the value at the end is not equal to zero.

    • Payment Type, one or zero, which indicates whether the payment occurs at the beginning of the month (1) or the end of the month (0).

12. Format the cells as desired. Figure 18-6 displays an example.

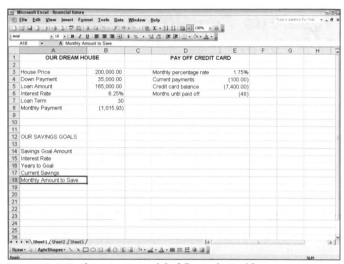

Figure 18-5: Reach your savings goals by following the Excel function

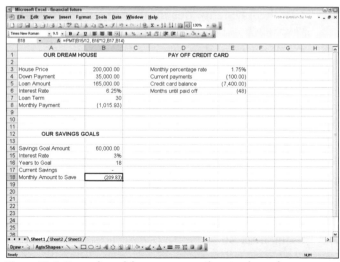

Figure 18-6: Format the worksheet so you can easily review the numbers

Integrating Excel into Word

*N*o single computer program does everything. You probably use multiple applications for different tasks, such as playing Solitaire, surfing the Internet, reading e-mail, and of course, working with Excel. If you use Excel, you probably use Microsoft Word to handle creating memos, letters, and other such documents.

In this chapter, I show you how to integrate two major Microsoft Office applications: Word and Excel. You discover how you can create a worksheet in Excel and include it in the middle of a Word document.

If you begin by creating a table in Word, then conclude that you are better off working with Excel, you also see how you copy the Word table into any Excel worksheet. There's no need to completely start over.

Copy Excel Cells into Word

1. From the Excel worksheet, highlight the cells you want to copy into a Word document. Choose Edit⇨Copy.

2. Open a Word document. Make sure the blinking cursor is at the location where you want the cells.

3. Choose Edit⇨Paste. Excel pastes the cells into a Word table. Figure 19-1 shows both the Excel worksheet and the new Word table.

 The Word table includes any Excel formatting such as column width, font, color, and border style.

 The Word table and the Excel worksheet are not linked together. Any changes made to one don't reflect on the other.

4. Modify the Word table using any of the following:

   - **Replace a value:** Highlight any existing text in a cell and type the replacement text.

   - **Delete a column or row:** Click in a cell of the column or row you want to delete and choose Table⇨Delete⇨Columns or Table⇨Delete⇨Rows.

   - **Insert rows or columns:** Click in a table cell where you want the new row or column and choose Table⇨Insert. Then select Columns to the Left, Columns to the Right, Rows Above, or Rows Below.

   - **Widen a column:** Position the mouse at the line to the right of any column and drag to the left or right.

   - **Delete the table from the Word document:** Select the row above the table, the table itself, and the row below the table and press the Delete key (see Figure 19-2).

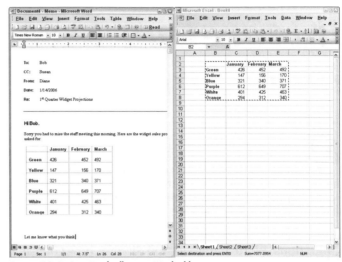

Figure 19-1: Copy Excel cells into a Word table

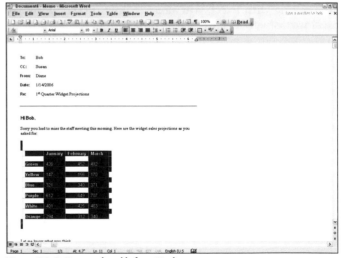

Figure 19-2: Remove the table from Word

Insert a Saved Excel Worksheet into Word

1. In a Word document, position the insertion point where you want the worksheet to appear.

2. Choose Insert⇨Object. The Object dialog box opens.

3. From the Create from File tab, click the Browse button. The Browse dialog box opens.

4. Locate and double-click the Excel file you want to include in your Word document. The Object dialog box reappears (see Figure 19-3).

5. Click OK. The Excel workbook appears as a Word table.

 Even if your worksheet contains multiple sheets, only the top sheet with all cells containing data appear. You cannot specify a particular range of cells. If you want an Excel chart, save the workbook with the chart on top before inserting into Word.

Edit the Inserted Worksheet

1. Click once on the Word table.

2. Perform one of the following actions:

   • Press Delete to delete the table.

   • Drag one of the handles to resize the table.

   • Double-click to edit the values. The Excel menu bar appears, along with column letters and row numbers. (See Figure 19-4.) The worksheet includes any formulas you created in Excel.

3. Click outside the table to deselect the table.

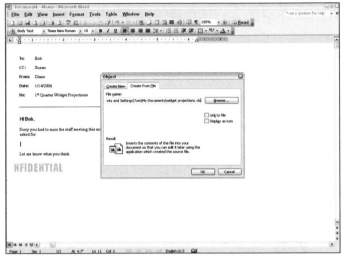

Figure 19-3: Insert a worksheet as an object

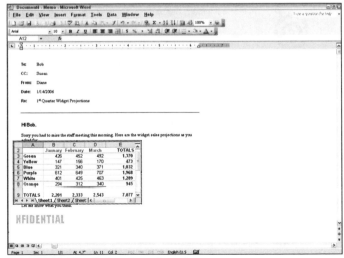

Figure 19-4: Edit cells, formulas, or formatting

Embed an Excel Worksheet into Word

1. Follow Steps 1 through 4 of the "Insert an Existing Worksheet into Word" section.

2. Click the Link to File option in the Object dialog box, shown in Figure 19-5. Click OK. The Excel workbook appears as a Word table. The Word table is linked to the original Excel worksheet.

Figure 19-5: Insert an Embedded worksheet into a Word document

 If you click Display as Icon, instead of displaying the workbook as a table, Word inserts an Excel icon into the document. Double-clicking the icon opens the workbook in Excel. However, the Excel program must be installed on the PC trying to open the workbook.

 To resize the Word table, click once on the table, which displays the eight sizing handles, and drag any handle until the table reaches the size you want.

 To delete the table, click once on the table and press the Delete key.

3. Make changes in the Excel workbook and the Word document using any of the following methods:

   • With the Word document open, right-click the Word table and choose Update Link.

   • Double-click the Word table, which launches the Excel program and opens the linked workbook (see Figure 19-6). Make any changes in Excel; the Word table automatically updates.

   • When you reopen the Word document, a dialog box prompts you to update the Word document from the original Excel file. Click Yes.

Figure 19-6: Changes in the original Excel workbook appear in the Word table

Copy a Word Table to Excel

1. In Microsoft Word, create a table (choose Table⇨ Insert⇨Table).

2. Enter any desired data in the Word table.

    Press Tab to move from cell to cell, or click the mouse in any individual cell.

3. Drag across the table to highlight the cells you want to copy, as shown in Figure 19-7.

4. Choose Edit⇨Copy or press Ctrl+C.

    To move, instead of copy, the Word table to Excel, choose Edit⇨ Cut or press Ctrl+X.

5. Open or create the Excel workbook in which you want to place the Word table.

6. Click the cell in which you want the table to begin.

7. Choose Edit⇨Paste or press Ctrl+V. The Excel worksheet displays the Word table. As shown in Figure 19-8, each cell in the Word table occupies one cell in the Excel worksheet.

    If the Word table cells have a border around them, the Excel cells also have a border around them.

    The Word table and the Excel worksheet are not linked together. Any changes made to one don't reflect on the other.

8. Format the cells as desired. See Chapter 4.

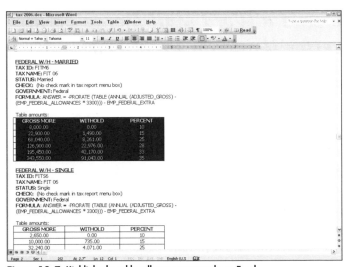

Figure 19-7: Highlight the table cells you want to take to Excel

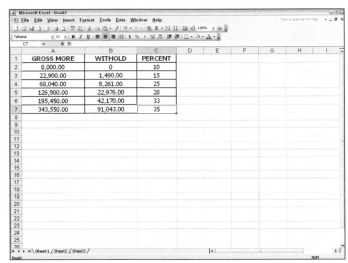

Figure 19-8: Copy a table from Word to Excel

Create a Word Mail Merge Form Letter Using an Excel List

1. Create and save an Excel worksheet with the data you want to merge in an Excel list. The Excel worksheet does not need to be open.

    Although not a requirement, the data will be easier for you to identify later if it has column headings.

2. In Word, choose Tools⇨Letters and Mailings⇨Mail Merge. The Mail Merge task pane appears on the right side (see Figure 19-9).

3. Select the Letters option.

4. Click Next: Starting Document.

5. Choose whether to create the mail merge from the current Word document or an existing Word document.

6. Click Next: Select Recipients.

7. Select the Use an Existing List option.

8. Click Browse. The Select Data Source dialog box appears.

9. Double-click the Excel file containing your list. The Select Table dialog box opens, as shown in Figure 19-10.

10. Select the range name, sheet name, or area containing data.

     If the first row of your list does not contain headers, remove the check from the First Row of Data Contains Colomn Headers option.

Figure 19-9: Select a mail merge document type

Figure 19-10: Select the data area you want to merge

11. Click OK. A Mail Merge Recipients list like the one in Figure 19-11 appears, containing your data.

12. Remove the check mark next to any record you don't want to include. Click OK.

 Optionally, click Clear All to clear all the check marks or click Select All to check all the records.

13. Click Next: Write Your Letter.

14. Type the form letter document, leaving blanks where you want the variable (such as name, address, phone number, or product) information to appear.

15. Click the insertion point at the first location where you want the variable information (such as the recipient name and address location).

16. From the task pane, select the desired option:

- **Address Block**: Select an address layout.

- **Greeting Line**: Insert a greeting of your choice, along with the recipient's first name (if you have such a field in your database), and then a comma or colon.

- **Electronic Postage**: Prints electronic postage on your envelopes (if you subscribe to an electronic postage service).

- **Postal Bar Code**: Prompts you for the zip code field from your Excel list and inserts a bar code matching the zip code field.

- **More Items**: Displays the Insert Merge Field dialog box (see Figure 19-12), which displays each field listed in your Excel list. Click the field you want to insert into Word, and click the Insert button.

Figure 19-11: Deselect any unwanted record

Figure 19-12: Select the fields you want included in the mail merge

17. Click Next: Preview Your Letters. As shown in Figure 19-13, the document you created appears with the first data record from your Excel list.

 Click through the Forward and Back buttons to browse through each recipient in your list. If you find a recipient you don't want to include, click the Exclude This Recipient button.

18. Click Next: Complete the Merge. You can now print your form letters.

 To edit a specific letter, click Edit Individual Letters. To make a change to the master document, click the Previous button until you get to Step 4, and then make any desired changes. Click the Next button until the merge is completed.

Make Mailing Labels

1. Follow Steps 1 and 2 from the previous section.

2. Select the Labels option and click Next: Starting Document.

3. Click Label Options. The Label Options dialog box, shown in Figure 19-14, appears.

4. Choose the label size and click OK. You see a blank document with label gridlines.

5. Click Next: Select Recipients. Follow Steps 7 through 12 of the previous section.

6. Click Next: Arrange Your Labels. On the first label, either insert the Address Block or individual fields.

7. Click the Update All Labels button. The fields you inserted appear on each label.

8. Click Next: Preview Your Labels. Each record appears on its own label.

9. Click Next: Complete the Merge. Print your labels.

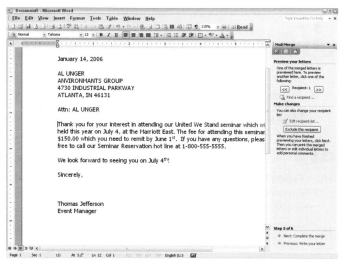

Figure 19-13: Preview the merged Excel list in the Word document file

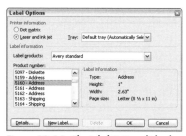

Figure 19-14: The Label Options dialog box

Blending Excel and PowerPoint

*O*ne of the most common ways to make others aware of your work is by giving a presentation. The Microsoft Office product, PowerPoint, is one of the most effective presentation products available in today's market. And because PowerPoint is part of the Microsoft Office suite, it's very easy to integrate information from other Office applications — in this example, Excel — into a PowerPoint presentation.

My mother always told me to do things right the first time. If you already spent the time and energy to create information in Excel, why should you have to re-create it in your PowerPoint presentation? You don't.

That's what this chapter is about. You find out how to take the powerful worksheet data or creative chart that you created in Excel and copy it to a PowerPoint slide. You can simply copy it once from Excel to PowerPoint, or you can create a link so that if the data in Excel changes, your PowerPoint presentation automatically reflects the changes. That's doing it right the first time.

Get ready to . . .

Copy Excel Cells into a PowerPoint Slide

1. From the Excel worksheet, highlight the cells you want to copy (see Figure 20-1). Choose Edit⇨Copy. A marquee appears around the highlighted cells.

2. Open a PowerPoint presentation. Make sure you display the slide on which you want to paste the cells.

3. Choose Edit⇨Paste or press Ctrl+V. Excel pastes the cells into a PowerPoint table including any formatting.

    The PowerPoint table and the Excel worksheet are not linked together. Any changes made to one don't reflect on the other.

4. Modify the PowerPoint table using any of the following:

   - **Replace a value:** Highlight any existing text in a cell and type the replacement text.

   - **Delete a row:** Click in the row you want to delete, right-click, and choose Delete Rows.

   - **Delete a column:** Highlight the column you want to delete, right-click, and choose Delete Columns.

   - **Change a column width:** Position the mouse at the invisible boundary line (as shown in Figure 20-2) to the right of any column and drag to the left or right.

   - **Delete the table from the slide:** Click once to select the table object (the table object boundary has striped edges) and click again on the table object boundary and press the Delete key.

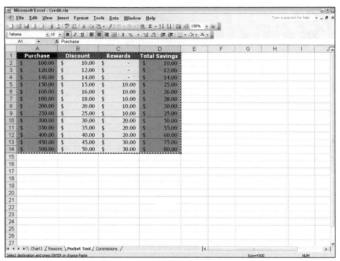

Figure 20-1: Use your favorite Copy command to duplicate cells

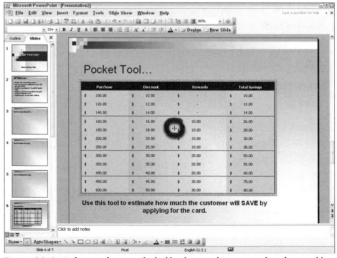

Figure 20-2: Make sure the cursor looks like this in order to resize the column widths

Drag an Excel Chart into a PowerPoint Slide

1. Open both the PowerPoint presentation you want to use and the Excel workbook that contains the chart. Make sure to display the PowerPoint slide you want.

2. Resize and arrange the PowerPoint and Excel windows so that both are visible at the same time. Use either of the following methods:

   - Right-click a blank area of the Windows taskbar and choose Tile Windows Vertically or Tile Windows Horizontally.

   - Click the Restore button in each window so they are no longer maximized. Drag the window borders to resize them and drag the title bars to move them until both windows are in the desired size and location.

3. Select the Excel chart you want to copy.

4. Hold Ctrl and drag the chart from the Excel window until it is in the PowerPoint slide. As you drag the mouse, the pointer looks like a small box as in Figure 20-3.

    If you want to *move* the chart from Excel to PowerPoint, instead of copying it, don't press Ctrl. Dragging an object without Ctrl moves the object.

5. Release the mouse button. The Excel chart appears on the PowerPoint slide, as shown in Figure 20-4.

6. Maximize the PowerPoint window to restore it to full screen. You can then resize or edit the chart as desired.

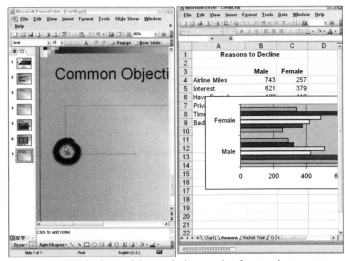

Figure 20-3: Use the drag-and-drop method to copy data from Excel to PowerPoint

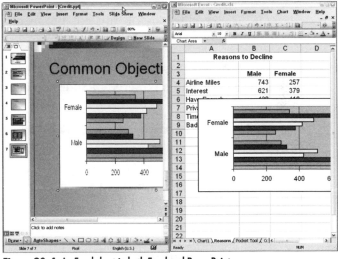

Figure 20-4: An Excel chart in both Excel and PowerPoint

Insert a Saved Excel Worksheet or Chart into a PowerPoint Slide

1. In PowerPoint, display the slide you want the worksheet or chart to appear on.

    If you want to copy a chart, make sure to save the workbook with the chart as the top sheet. If your workbook contains multiple worksheets, only the top sheet appears in the PowerPoint slide.

2. Choose Insert➪Object. The Insert Object dialog box opens (see Figure 20-5).

3. Click the Create from File option.

4. Click the Browse button. The Browse dialog box opens.

5. Double-click the Excel file you want to include. The Object dialog box reappears and the path and filename appear in the File text box.

6. Click OK. The Excel workbook or chart appears on the current PowerPoint slide, as shown in Figure 20-6.

7. Modify the PowerPoint table or chart with any of the following methods (or check out the earlier section "Copy Excel Cells into a PowerPoint Slide" for additional ways):

    Any changes are saved in PowerPoint only, not in the original Excel workbook.

   - Click once on the PowerPoint object. Drag a handle to resize the object.

   - Double-click the table or chart to edit the actual values. The Excel menu bar appears, along with column letters and row numbers.

Figure 20-5: Inserting data from a previously saved Excel workbook

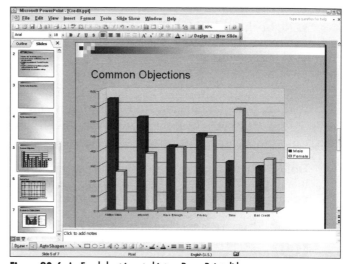

Figure 20-6: An Excel chart inserted into a PowerPoint slide

Link an Excel Worksheet into a PowerPoint Slide

1. Open the desired Excel file. When creating a link, the originating Excel file must be a previously saved file.

2. Select the portion of the file you want to duplicate in PowerPoint.

3. Choose Edit⇨Copy or press Ctrl+C.

4. Display the PowerPoint slide on which you want to create the link and choose Edit⇨Paste Special, which displays the Paste Special dialog box (see Figure 20-7).

5. Choose the Paste Link option. With this option selected, any changes you make to the original workbook reflect in the PowerPoint slide each time you open the PowerPoint presentation.

 If you click Display as Icon, PowerPoint inserts an Excel icon onto the slide. Double-clicking the icon opens the workbook in Excel. The PC opening the workbook must have Excel installed.

6. Click OK. The linked object appears on the slide.

7. Refresh Excel data in PowerPoint by one of these methods:

   • With the PowerPoint presentation open, right-click the PowerPoint table and choose Update Link (see Figure 20-8).

   • Double-click the PowerPoint table, which opens the linked workbook in Excel. Changes in Excel automatically update in the PowerPoint table.

   • When you reopen the PowerPoint presentation, a dialog box prompts you to update PowerPoint from the original Excel file. Click Yes.

Figure 20-7: The PowerPoint Paste Special dialog box

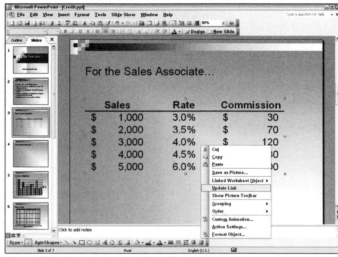

Figure 20-8: Updating the PowerPoint slide object

Using Excel with Access

*Y*ou can share data between Access and Excel in many ways. You can copy data from an open worksheet and paste it into an Access data-sheet, import a worksheet into an Access database, or simply load an Access datasheet into Excel using the Analyze It with Excel command.

This chapter shows you how to exchange data between Access and Excel through one of several processes:

➥ Importing, which creates a copy of an Excel spreadsheet in Access format.

➥ Linking, which connects an Access table to an Excel worksheet. You can view and edit the data in both the original program and in the Access file. Linking is useful when you need to share Excel data between Excel and Access users.

➥ Exporting, which lets you analyze your Access data in Excel format.

This chapter assumes you already know general database terms, such as records, fields, tables, queries, and primary keys. I also assume you know the basics of creating and using an Access database.

Get ready to . . .

Copy Data from Excel to an Access Table

1. If you don't already have an Access database created, from Access, choose File⇨New. If you already have an Access database, open the database and skip Steps 2 and 3.

2. From the task pane, click Blank Database. The File New Database window appears.

3. Enter a name and location for the new database and click Create.

4. Switch to the Excel worksheet that contains the data you want to copy.

 You cannot save an Excel worksheet as an Access database and you cannot create a link to Access from within Excel.

5. Highlight the cells you want to copy to Access. Be sure to include headings if you have them, as shown in Figure 21-1.

6. Choose Edit⇨Copy.

7. Switch to the Access database.

8. Choose Edit⇨Paste.

9. Click Yes if you included column headings in Step 5. A completion message box appears.

 If you included headings, Access uses those headings as field names in the table.

10. Click OK. Access creates a new table in the database (see Figure 21-2).

Figure 21-1: Select the cells you want to copy

Figure 21-2: An Access table named after the Excel worksheet tab

Import Data from Excel to an Access Table

1. Prepare your Excel worksheet data before importing:

   - If you don't want to import the entire worksheet, in the Excel workbook, create a named range containing the cells that you want to import. (See Chapter 2.)

   - Make sure the cells are in tabular format. If the worksheet contains merged cells, then the contents of the cell are placed in the field that corresponds to the leftmost column, and the other fields are left blank.

   - If the Excel spreadsheet has a cell containing more than 255 characters, and the cell is in a row farther than row 25, move the row up in the Excel list so it's within the first 25 records. Otherwise, Access truncates the data to 255 characters.

2. If you don't already have an Access database created, from Access, choose File⇨New. If you already have an Access database, open the database and skip Steps 3 and 4.

3. From the task pane, click Blank Database. The File New Database window appears (see Figure 21-3).

4. Enter a name and location for the new database and click Create.

5. Choose File⇨Get External Data⇨Import. The Import dialog box appears.

6. Select Microsoft Excel from the Files of Type drop-down list, as shown in Figure 21-4.

7. Select the Excel file from which you want to import data.

 Importing a worksheet into Access creates a duplicate copy of the data and does not make any changes to the source Excel file.

Figure 21-3: Create a new database for importing Excel data

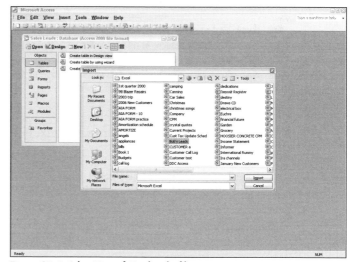

Figure 21-4: Select Microsoft Excel as the file type you want to import

8. Click the Import button. The Import Spreadsheet Wizard appears (see Figure 21-5).

9. Select whether to import the entire spreadsheet or a range. If the spreadsheet has no named ranges and only one worksheet, you do not see this screen. Click Next.

10. Specify whether the first row of your worksheet contains column headings. If it does, Access creates field names from the first row. If it doesn't, you can assign field names in Step 12. Click Next.

11. Specify whether you want the data in an existing table or a new table. If you want the data in an existing table, you need to select the table name. Click Next.

If you select an existing table, Access appends the data to the table. Make the sure the number of columns in the worksheet or named range matches the number of fields in the table. The name, date type, and position of each column must also match those of the corresponding field in the Access table.

12. Assign field names to each column by clicking each column and typing a name in the Field Name text box. (See Figure 21-6.)

If a column name violates the field naming rules in Access, Access assigns a valid name to the field.

13. Choose Yes or No if you want the field indexed. Click Next.

Optionally, click on a column you don't want to include and click the Do Not Import Field (Skip) option. You can skip columns during the import, but you can't skip rows.

Figure 21-5: Choose the area you want to import

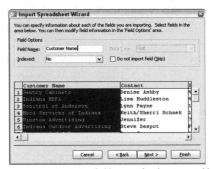

Figure 21-6: Assign field names for the Access table

14. Select an option for the primary index key. You can either let Access create one for you, select your own primary key or not have a primary key at all. Click Next.

15. Enter a name for the Access table.

16. Click Finish. Access imports the data and displays a message box like the one in Figure 21-7.

 If any errors incur during the import, Access creates an error log table in the database and displays the name of the table in the message. It's a good idea to open the error log table and review the errors.

17. Click OK. Access creates the table (see Figure 21-8).

 To import multiple worksheets or named ranges, repeat the import process for each worksheet or range.

18. Review the imported data. Keep the following items in mind:

- **Graphical elements**: Access does not import graphical elements, such as logos, charts, and pictures.

- **Data type:** Access determines the data type based on the first 25 rows of data. If any values beyond the 25th row are not compatible with the chosen data type, Access ignores those values and does not import them.

 You cannot change the data type of the destination field during the import operation, but you can change data types from the Access table design.

- **Calculated values:** Access imports only the results of a calculated cell, not the formula itself. If you need the formulas to update, you need to link the Excel worksheet to Access.

- **Hyperlinks:** Access imports cells containing hyperlinks as text fields.

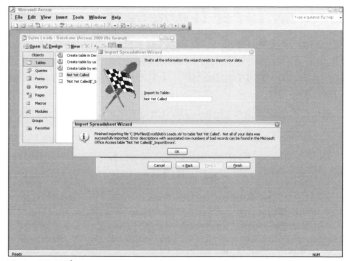

Figure 21-7: The import status message

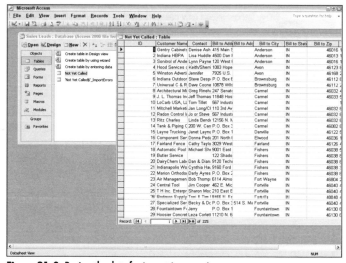

Figure 21-8: Review the data for import inaccuracies

Link an Excel Worksheet to an Access Database

1. Begin by applying Steps 1 through 4 of the previous section.

2. Choose File➪Open. The Open dialog box appears.

3. From the Files of Type list box, select Microsoft Excel.

4. Locate and select the Excel worksheet you want to link to Access (see Figure 21-9).

5. Click the Open button. Access creates a blank database named with the Excel filename, and automatically starts the Link Spreadsheet Wizard.

6. Select which worksheet or named range you want to link. If the spreadsheet has no named ranges and only a single worksheet, you do not see this screen.

 You can import only one worksheet or named range at a time. To link multiple worksheets or named ranges, repeat the link operation.

7. Click Next.

8. Specify whether the first row of your worksheet contains column headings (see Figure 21-10). If there are headings, Access creates field names from the first row. If not, Access assumes the first row is a record.

9. Click Next. Enter a name for the table.

10. Click Create.

11. Click Finish. A completion message box appears.

12. Click OK.

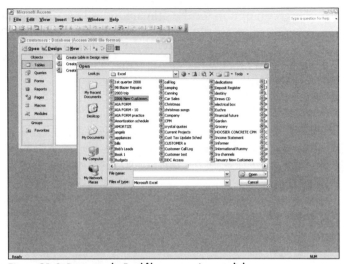

Figure 21-9: Determine the Excel file you want Access to link

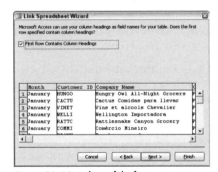

Figure 21-10: Indicate if the first row contains column headings

13. Double-click the Access table that appears as an Excel icon with an arrow next to it (as shown in Figure 21-11). Keep the following in mind when reviewing the data in Access:

- Graphics, such as logos, charts or pictures, stored in the Excel worksheet, are not visible in Access.

- You cannot change the field data type or size.

- The source cells that contain formulas display only as results in Access, but you cannot modify the values in Access.

- Access stores Excel cells longer than 255 characters in a memo field that displays only the first 255 characters.

 If you delete the table from Access, you're deleting only the link, not the actual Excel worksheet.

Analyze Access Data with Microsoft Excel

1. Open the Access database you want to analyze.

2. Select the datasheet, form, or report you want to analyze.

3. Choose Tools⇨Office Links⇨Analyze It with Microsoft Excel. The datasheet opens in Microsoft Excel as an Excel worksheet. Figure 21-12 shows both the Access form and the Excel worksheet.

 Access saves the datasheet as an Excel file in the same location as the Access file. If a file already exists with that name, Access prompts you to overwrite the existing file. If you choose not to, then Access prompts you for a filename and location.

 The worksheet is not linked to Access. Any changes made to the Excel worksheet do not appear in the Access datasheet.

Figure 21-11: An Excel linked icon in an Access database

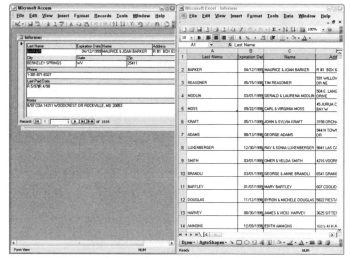

Figure 21-12: Review the Access data in an independent Excel workbook

Export Access Data to Excel

1. Open the Access database and select the database object that you want to export. (See Figure 21-13.) The following table illustrates what Access exports, depending on the object and the view you have open when performing the export.

 You can export only an Access table, query, form, or report. You cannot export data Access pages, macros, or modules.

Object	View	What Exports
Tables, Queries, or Forms	Database window	Everything unless you pre-select an area before exporting.
Form	Form view	All fields and records even if the fields aren't included in the view.
Report	Database window, Print Preview, or Layout Preview	All data Group Header and Detail text boxes, and any text box in a Group Footer that has a Sum function. Access uses Excel's Outline feature.

2. Choose File⇨Export. The Export To dialog box shown in Figure 21-14 appears.

3. In the Save as Type box, choose Microsoft Excel 97-2003.

4. From the Save In box, select a location in which to save the file, as shown in Figure 21-15.

5. In the File Name box, enter a name for the file. By default, Access suggests the Access object name.

Figure 21-13: Select the Access object you want to export

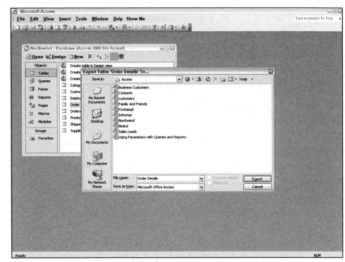

Figure 21-14: The Export To dialog box

6. Optionally, if you are exporting a table or a query, click the Save Formatted check box, which tells Access to also export the field formatting. If the filename you selected in Step 5 already exists, one of the following occurs:

- If you don't select the option, and the filename you choose already exists, Access doesn't overwrite the file; it adds a new worksheet to the file with the same name as the object that is being exported.

- If you select the option and export a table, the Excel worksheet takes on formatting similar to the Access table, but overwrites the existing worksheet contents.

- If you select the option and if you export an Access form or report, Access overwrites the Excel workbook by removing the original worksheets, and creating a new worksheet with the same name as the exported object.

7. Click the Export button or, if you want to export only a pre-selected datasheet portion, click Save Selection. Additionally, the following actions occur during the export:

- Graphic items such as images do not export.

- Only calculation results export, not the calculation itself.

- Check boxes on forms do not export.

- Subreports export, but subforms do not.

- Date values earlier than Jan 1, 1900, do not export and are replaced with a Null value.

8. Open the Excel worksheet and validate the export feature. (See Figure 21-16.) For example, if a value was Null in Access, during the export, the values might be replaced with the data that should be in the adjacent column in the resulting worksheet.

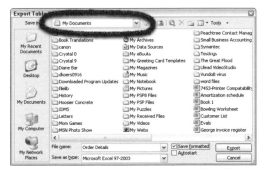

Figure 21-15: Select a location for the exported Excel file

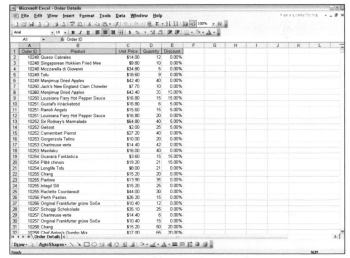

Figure 21-16: Export some or all of the Access data to Excel

Index

• *G* •

• *H* •

• I •

• L •

• M •

• N •

• O •

• *R* •

• Z •

Notes